THE GREAT WAR

A PICTORIAL HISTORY

THE GREAT WAR

A PICTORIAL HISTORY

DUNCAN HILL

PHOTOGRAPHS BY
Daily Mail

Published by Atlantic Publishing

38 Copthorne Road, Croxley Green
Hertfordshire, WD3 4AQ, UK

© Atlantic Publishing 2013
Photographs and facsimile reports © Associated Newspapers Archive

A catalogue record for this book is available from the British Library.

Hardback ISBN: 978-1-909242-57-9
Paperback ISBN: 978-1-909242-14-2
Also available in paperback in the USA from Welcome Rain ISBN: 978-1-56649-392-5

Printed and bound in China

Introduction

'The lamps are going out all over Europe. We shall not see them lit again in our lifetime.' So said British Foreign Secretary Sir Edward Grey on the eve of the Great War in 1914. The assassination of Archduke Franz Ferdinand was the event that plunged the continent into darkness for four long years, but it was merely the catalyst to a long-expected confrontation between Europe's two great power blocs. It had been 40 years since the major powers had taken to the battlefield, and there were many keen to show their might and mettle. The grim realities of trench warfare made a mockery of Germany's intention to deliver a speedy knockout blow to Britain and France, then look east to its Russian foe. This would be an attritional conflict marked by catastrophic loss of life, often for marginal territorial gain. Places such as Ypres, Verdun, Gallipoli and the Somme would forever become bywords for industrial-scale slaughter.

The Great War: A Pictorial History uses contemporaneous reports and photographs from the *Daily Mail* archives, including many eyewitness accounts, to show how the conflicts of that period developed, describing the key battles, tactical decisions and turning points that settled the outcome.

Setting the stage for war

By the summer of 1914, the tensions between the great powers of Europe had been mounting for some time. The continent was divided into shifting power blocs and rival ruling dynasties, and the decline of the Ottoman Empire, which had once extended across Europe from Turkey to just outside Vienna, added to the instability.

The fact that the rulers of Great Britain, Germany and Russia were first cousins did not do anything to reduce the levels of tension. In Britain, George V, the second son of Edward VII, had acceded to the throne in 1910. Tsar Nicholas II had ruled over the vast Russian Empire since 1894, and the German Empire was headed by Kaiser Wilhelm II, who had succeeded the Iron Chancellor, Otto von Bismarck, in 1888. The Dual Monarchy of Austria–Hungary had been ruled by the Habsburg Emperor Franz Josef I since 1867 and France was a Republic, led by Raymond Poincaré.

Alliances

National security was a critical issue for all of the major states; the developing tensions meant that no nation felt secure by itself, each of them needing allies on whom they could depend. In 1879 Germany and Austria-Hungary had formed an alliance. They were joined by Italy because of its historic antipathy towards France. In response, Russia and France clubbed together by signing the Double Entente in 1894.

Britain had yet to decide on its position. London was suspicious of the growing might of Germany, but had clashed with France as recently as 1898 over a territorial dispute in the Sudan. In the event, Britain sided with France. King Edward VII had charmed the French public during a state visit in May 1903 and the two countries signed the 'Entente Cordiale' within the year. It was not a formal alliance, but a friendly understanding, and neither country was under any obligation to support the other in time of war. In August 1907, Britain further cemented its commitment to France by signing an agreement with Russia. Europe was divided into two powerful blocs.

ABOVE: **British soldiers going over the top at Arras, April 1917.**

LEFT: **Unaware that one of the greatest wars of all time was about to start, a British family at Waterloo Station set off on their summer holidays.**

OPPOSITE TOP RIGHT: **Kaiser Wilhelm II ascended to the German throne in 1888 and quickly cast aside the shrewd 'Iron Chancellor', Otto von Bismarck. He replaced Bismarck's conservative foreign policy, which had emphasized diplomacy and an avoidance of conflict, with a rash and belligerent quest for glory.**

OPPOSITE LEFT: **Kaiser Wilhelm with his cousin King George V of Great Britain. Both were grandchildren of Queen Victoria.**

OPPOSITE MIDDLE RIGHT: **Russia's Tsar Nicholas II and his family pictured shortly before the war. Russia's decision to stand with Serbia against Austria-Hungary led to the outbreak of the First World War.**

OPPOSITE BOTTOM: **A young Winston Churchill, then First Lord of the Admiralty, is pictured after taking a 60-mile flight from Upavon to Portsmouth in the summer of 1914.**

Arms race

For centuries the powers of Europe had clashed over their competing interests around the globe. During the nineteenth century, they usually reverted to diplomacy to resolve their differences, but in the early twentieth century the network of alliances emboldened both sides and diplomatic responses soon gave way to militaristic ones. To adjust to the aggressive new order of international relations each of the powers began rapidly building up their arsenals, for it had become clear that the brawniest power would get its way.

Europe was presented with four major crises between 1905 and 1913, two between France and Germany over Morocco and two between Austria-Hungary and Russia over the Balkans, but each time neither side felt sufficiently comfortable in their arsenals to risk war. However, the situation had changed by the time a fresh crisis emerged in the Balkans in 1914. On this occasion, neither side was willing to back down because both thought they could win.

Assassination in Sarajevo

Archduke Franz Ferdinand, the 51-year-old nephew of Franz Josef and heir to the Habsburg throne, was on an official visit to Sarajevo in the summer of 1914. He was well aware of the potential danger as there had already been some assassination attempts by disaffected Bosnian Serbs, who were opposed to Austrian rule in Bosnia and sought to include the region in a wider Serbian state. However, he hoped to win over the locals with a well publicized trip through the streets of Sarajevo. This gave members of the Serbian nationalist Black Hand organization the perfect opportunity to strike a blow against their Austro-Hungarian oppressors.

When the visit took place on June 28, a seven-strong assassination squad was lying in wait. However, the assassination attempt failed when the bomb that was to be thrown into the Archduke's car missed its target and exploded in the street. The Archduke decided to carry on with his official visit, which gave the assassins a second chance to strike. One of them, 19-year-old Gavrilo Princip, assuming their efforts had failed had gone to have lunch in a Sarajevo café. Luck was on his side; the Archduke's driver had taken a wrong turn and stopped to turn around close to the café. Seizing his opportunity, Princip turned his pistol on the car's occupants. Franz Ferdinand was hit in the neck and his wife Sophie, who was expecting their fourth child, in the stomach. Both of them were quickly pronounced dead.

DAILY MAIL   JUNE 29, 1914

Murder of the Austrian heir and his wife

We regret to state that the Archduke Francis Ferdinand, the heir to the throne of Austria-Hungary, and his morganatic wife, the Duchess of Hohenberg, were assassinated yesterday.

The assassination took place at Sarajevo, the capital of Bosnia, which State, together with Herzegovina, was annexed by Austria-Hungary from Turkey in 1908. Bosnia, which is bounded on the south by Montenegro and Servia, has a large Slav population that is discontented with Austrian rule.

The Archduke had paid no heed to warnings to him not to go to Bosnia on account of the disturbed state of the province. Anti-Austrian demonstrations were made before his arrival at Sarajevo on Saturday. Two attempts were made to kill the Archduke and his wife at Sarajevo yesterday. The first failed; the second was only too successful.

A 21-year-old printer of Servian nationality living in Herzegovina threw a bomb at the Archduke's motor-car in the street. The Archduke deflected the bomb with his arm. It fell to the ground and exploded. The heir to the throne and his wife escaped, but a number of other people were injured, six of them seriously.

A little while later the Archduke and his wife were driving to see the victims of the bomb explosion, when a schoolboy aged 19, apparently also of Servian nationality, threw at them a bomb which, however, did not explode, and then fired at them with a Browning automatic pistol. Both were wounded and both died shortly afterwards.

Igniting the war

The Austro–Hungarian empire was outraged by the murders, but it wanted more than mere revenge; this was an ideal opportunity to crush Serbia and also consolidate an empire that was in danger of breaking apart. Russia had strong historic ties to Serbia, but had backed down from supporting Belgrade in the two previous Balkan crises. However, Russia had since built up its military, with French assistance, and on this occasion was prepared to stand with Serbia against Austria-Hungary.

Austria-Hungary looked to Germany for support. Berlin had realized that it would soon be outpaced in the arms race by the Entente powers and that the window in which it could win a war was rapidly closing. As a result, the German Kaiser confirmed his full support for Franz Josef's government. On July 31 Germany issued Russia with an ultimatum: to cease any mobilization immediately. No reply came, and the following day Germany declared war on its large eastern neighbour. The Great War had begun.

DAILY MAIL JULY 25, 1914

European crisis

Russia, apparently on the appeal of Servia, intervened yesterday in the crisis with Austria.

Causes of the Crisis.- The Austrian heir and his wife were murdered on June 28 at Sarajevo, capital of the Austrian province of Bosnia, by a Servian sympathiser. Servians are Slavs (i.e. of kin with Russians). Most of the Bosnians are Slavs. Pan-Servians dream of a 'Greater Servia' to include Austrian Slavs. Bulgaria is a Slav Czardom.

Austrian Demands.- Austria has made 10 demands on Servia. The chief are:

1. A reply by 6 p.m. to-night.
2. Punishment of Servian accomplices in the assassinations at Sarajevo.
3. An end to 'Greater Servia' plots against Austria.
4. The publication in the front page of the Servian official journal to-day of an official apology for and condemnation of 'Greater Servia' dreams.

Count Berchtold, the Austrian Foreign Minister, to-day goes to Ischl, where the Emperor is, to await the Servian reply. If a satisfactory reply has not been given by 6 p.m. to-night the Austrian Minister in Belgrade, the Servian capital, has been ordered to leave Servia.

TOP LEFT: **Archduke Ferdinand and his wife alight from their car at Sarajevo city hall after the first failed assassination attempt.**

ABOVE LEFT: **The Archduke and his wife leave a reception at city hall. A wrong turn on the way to their next engagement results in their assassination.**

TOP RIGHT: **Archduke Franz Ferdinand and his family. His marriage was morganatic, which meant his children could not inherit the throne of Austria-Hungary.**

ABOVE RIGHT: **Crowds try to attack the assassin, Gavrilo Princip, as police lead him away.**

OPPOSITE: **A crowd forms outside the War Office in London waiting for news as to how Britain and France will respond to the outbreak of war between Russia and Germany.**

BRITISH ULTIMATUM TO GERMANY.

TO REPLY BY MIDNIGHT.

The Unsatisfactory Answers of Germany.

BELGIUM'S APPEAL.

In the House of Commons this afternoon Mr. Asquith announced the

SUMMARY OF TO-DAY'S WAR NEWS.

It is reported, but not confirmed, that German and French warships have fought off Flamborough Head.

Germany is stated to have declared that if she considers it essential she will break through Belgian territory by force of arms.

German troops are said to have invaded Belgium.

A German company is reported to have reached Mars-la-Tour.

The British Government have been informed officially that German troops are in Belgium. At noon to-day the German Embassy issued a statement that no troops had crossed the frontier.

A correspondent says that Belgium may interrupt German communications by flooding the country on their invasion route.

The Commander-in-Chief of the French Army is on his way to the frontier.

The Cabinet sat from 11.30

THE BULLYING OF BELGIUM.

Germany Prepared to Carry Through "Essential Measures" by Force of Arms.

AEROPLANE BOMBS.

FRENCH FRONTIER TOWN DAMAGED.

DAILY MAIL AUGUST 3, 1914

Great war begun by Germany

The German Government declared war upon Russia at 7.30 on Saturday evening. There was still hope of peace when this action was taken. The Czar had pledged his word to the Kaiser that he would not mobilise or attack Austria while negotiations with her were in progress.

The German Army was active yesterday. It crossed the French frontier, without any declaration of war, at three distinct points. It invaded France at Longwy, 270 miles from London, close to the Luxemburg frontier; at Cirey, near Nancy; and at Delle, near Belfort.

German troops were last night in French territory.

BY THE KING.
A PROCLAMATION
REGARDING THE DEFENCE OF THE REALM.

GEORGE R.I.

WHEREAS by the law of Our Realm it is Our undoubted prerogative and the duty of all Our loyal subjects acting in Our behalf in times of imminent national danger to take all such measures as may be necessary for securing the public safety and the defence of Our Realm:

AND WHEREAS the present state of Public Affairs in Europe is such as to constitute an imminent national danger:

NOW, THEREFORE WE strictly command and enjoin Our subjects to obey and conform to all instructions and regulations which may be issued by Us or Our Admiralty or Army Council, or any officer of Our Navy or Army, or any other person acting in Our behalf for securing the objects aforesaid, and not to hinder or obstruct, but to afford all assistance in their power to any person acting in accordance with any such instructions or regulations or otherwise in the execution of any measures duly taken for securing those objects.

Given at Our Court at Buckingham Palace, this Fourth day of August, in the year of our Lord one thousand nine hundred and fourteen, and in the Fifth year of Our Reign.

GOD SAVE THE KING.

DAILY MAIL   AUGUST 3, 1914

British warning to Germany

We understand that an intimation has been conveyed to the German Government to the effect that if a single German soldier is ordered to set foot on Belgian soil the British Navy will take instant action against Germany.

Germany has also seized a British liner at Kiel and a British collier at Brunsbuettel, near the canal.

The German Emperor officially ordered a mobilisation of the entire forces of Germany at 5.15 yesterday afternoon. Actually the German mobilization had been secretly begun three days ago, on July 31.

The French Government ordered the mobilisation of all its forces to begin at midnight of Saturday-Sunday. In seven or eight days the French armies, with a strength of at least 1,000,000 men, will be ready to fight on the frontier. Behind them will be other armies ready to give them all support.

Italy has intimated that she will not support Germany and Austria. Her treaty of alliance with them does not compel her to fight in a war of aggression. She was only bound to intervene if Germany and Austria were attacked without provocation. Italian neutrality will be maintained by a general mobilisation of the Italian forces.

The Schlieffen Plan

The pent-up tensions of the previous years ensured that events moved very fast, and Germany knew that it was only a matter of time before France entered the war on the side of its Russian ally. A two-front war posed a serious threat, but the German general staff had developed a contingency measure. Called the Schlieffen Plan, it called for a rapid strike towards Paris to effectively neutralize the threat from France, after which the German army could turn its attention back to Russia. There was one critical factor for the Plan's success: speed. Russia's enormous size meant it would take time to gather enough troops to launch an attack, giving Germany a short time to act before it faced a real threat. France, therefore, had to be put out of action quickly so that the full strength of the German army could be in position on the eastern front before Russia was ready to fight. Accordingly, even before war was formally declared between Germany and France on August 3, German forces began the march westwards. The situation in the east was largely left to Austria–Hungary.

Under the Schlieffen Plan, the German attack on France would be made through Belgium, rather than directly across the Franco–German border. This was problematic because Belgium was a neutral country, and Britain was a long-standing guarantor of its neutrality. However, Germany was not certain that Britain would intervene because London was preoccupied with the question of Home Rule for Ireland and powerful members of Prime Minister Asquith's government were adamantly against Britain being drawn into any European conflict. Moreover, Britain was under no treaty obligation to take up arms in these circumstances.

Germany invades Belgium

Germany demanded unhindered passage through Belgium and, on August 3, the Belgian government rejected its ultimatum and looked to Britain for support. The Asquith government chose to honour its commitment to Belgium and did so unequivocally, to the astonishment of Theobald Bethmann-Hollweg, the German Chancellor. Britain refused to stand aside while Belgium and, eventually, France were invaded.

On August 4, London delivered an ultimatum to Germany, which expired at midnight: Britain would declare war if German forces failed to withdraw from Belgium. Midnight came and went with no response. Bethmann-Hollweg could barely believe it. 'Just for a scrap of paper Great Britain was going to make war on a kindred nation who desired nothing better than to be friends with her,' he declared. Germany had badly misjudged the situation. Many of the people in all the nations involved seem to have felt a kind of joy, even euphoria at this point. British Foreign Secretary Sir Edward Grey was far more perceptive when he stated 'The lamps are going out all over Europe; we shall not see them lit again in our lifetime'.

OPPOSITE MIDDLE:
Crowds cheer outside Buckingham Palace on the evening of August 4, 1914 after hearing of the declaration of war.

OPPOSITE INSET:
The Palace issues a proclamation regarding the defence of the Realm upon the outbreak of war on August 4, 1914.

OPPOSITE BOTTOM:
Crowds gather to watch Lord Gordon Lennox lead the 2nd Grenadier Guards past Buckingham Palace shortly after the outbreak of war.

OPPOSITE TOP RIGHT:
German soldiers in Berlin receive flowers as they march off to war.

TOP: **Young Britons march past the War Office in London to show their support for the newly declared war.**

ABOVE: **Onlookers watch as the sign is taken down from the door of the German Embassy in London.**

German successes

The Central Powers – the German and Austro–Hungarian forces – received early encouragement. The German army swept through Belgium quickly and Liege, the fortress town, fell. This was a strategic victory that was essential to the success of the Schlieffen Plan. The Belgian government left Brussels for Antwerp on August 17, and only three days later the country's capital was in German hands. There were reports of atrocities committed by the German troops. Though some of these were clearly exaggeration and propaganda, it soon became clear that the German army wanted more than simple surrender from the people it conquered. It intended to obliterate any obstacles in its path, crushing the spirit of its opponents as well as succeeding in battle. The cathedral town of Louvain was sacked in the closing days of August in a manner that shocked the world; the Germans claimed that shots had been fired against their soldiers, and many civilians paid the ultimate price in revenge. Additionally, Louvain's magnificent and unique university library, with its many priceless books and manuscripts, was destroyed. A month later the magnificent Gothic cathedral at Rheims suffered a terrible bombardment, even though a Red Cross flag was flying from it.

DAILY MAIL AUGUST 18, 1914

The British army in France

The British Expeditionary Force is in France. This news, officially promulgated to-day, discloses the great secret. The military authorities have accomplished a thrilling feat. With perfect secrecy they have mobilised, assembled in British ports, and moved to France the largest army that ever left British shores. We may justly congratulate them on their energy and organisation. They have worked in silence with admirable efficiency.

This is not the first time that a British army has gathered on French soil. But it is the first time that British troops have entered France to aid her. The cause for which that gallant army marches today is the same as that for which its forefathers fought in 1814 and 1815. It has gone forth to defend the right, to protect the weak against lawless attack, to uphold the great cause of human freedom against the onslaught of military despotism. It stands, as the England of 1814 stood, for liberty against tyranny. And in that fight, however protracted, however terrible, it will not quail. He was a wise French soldier who said that England, when she had once taken hold, never let go. Through whatever suffering and sacrifices this army which she has sent forth with all her love and faith will carry her standard to victory.

ABOVE LEFT: **British marines march through the Belgian coastal town of Ostend.**

BELOW: **Fallen soldiers following the Battle of the Marne.**

ABOVE: **Wounded soldiers arriving at Ostend, having failed to prevent the fall of Antwerp on October 9, 1914.**

The Battle of the Marne

However, Germany's initial success disguised major weaknesses; the army was overstretched and undersupplied. Russia went on the offensive in August and two German corps were redeployed east, just as the British Expeditionary Force began arriving to shore up French defences. Nevertheless, German troops were within striking distance of Paris and the Allies had to act quickly to save the French capital. The result was the Battle of the Marne, which took place in early September 1914. A great number of men were killed on both sides, but the battle resulted in a German retreat – their forces moving to a more easily defendable position on the high ground north of the Aisne river. Neither side could make further headway and a long war of attrition set in.

DAILY MAIL   AUGUST 22, 1914

German entry into Brussels

Brussels was unconditionally surrendered by the Burgomaster to a German advance guard. Germany has imposed a fine of £8,000,000 on the city of Brussels. A German force, 35,000 strong, with bands playing, marched into the city in the afternoon. The Germans behaved with brutal arrogance to the population and to captured Belgian officers.

The Belgians were heavily defeated, with great loss and the capture of 12 guns, by the Germans at Louvain on Wednesday. The Belgian troops offered a gallant resistance, but were overwhelmed by numbers.

ABOVE LEFT: **Lance-Corporal Charles Alfred Jarvis (second right) attempts to recruit men in Woodford Green, London. Jarvis became the first soldier of the war to be awarded the Victoria Cross, in recognition of his actions at Mons on August 23, 1914.**

LEFT: **Conscription was not introduced in Britain until 1916, but around 2,500,000 men volunteered for active service in Lord Kitchener's Army.**

TOP RIGHT: **The British head off to war. Less than three weeks after the outbreak of war, a 120,000 strong British Expeditionary Force stood on the Continent. They engaged the Germans in their first battle at Mons, Belgium, on August 23.**

ABOVE RIGHT: **Lord Kitchener (left), a veteran of the Boer War and the campaign in the Sudan in 1898, was appointed Secretary of State for War by Prime Minister Asquith at the outset of the confict.**

The Eastern Front

The Schlieffen Plan meant that Germany allocated minimal resources to the Russian Front in 1914. The Eighth Army, under the command of General Prittwitz, was sent to the east to hold the line while war was waged against France in the west. The Russian army was inferior to the Germans in terms of training and leadership, but vastly superior in terms of numbers. This caused Prittwitz to panic and order a partial retreat, so an angry government in Berlin replaced him with generals Hindenberg and Ludendorff.

In August 1914, the Russian generals planned to strike at the German Eighth Army, which was based to the west of the Masurian Lakes. The Russian First Army marched around the lakes to the north and the Second Army planned to approach from the south in order to trap the Germans in a classic pincer movement. However, things did not go according to plan because the Germans intercepted radio communication between the two armies. Knowing his troops were no match for both Russian armies, General Hindenberg marched to engage the Second Army while the First was too far away to come to their aid. The resulting battle near Tannenberg was a disaster for Russia; the Second Army was almost wiped out, 30,000 men were killed and 100,000 were taken prisoner.

ABOVE: **The remnants of the Russian Second Army in full-scale retreat after the crushing defeat at the Battle of Tannenberg.**

LEFT: **Russian soldiers march westwards. Although they were poorly trained and lacked equipment, the Russian army had strength in numbers.**

BELOW LEFT: **Troops on the Eastern Front face the harsh winter. Thousands would die during the conflict as a result of the cold.**

OPPOSITE TOP LEFT: **Downtime in the Russian ranks. Fighting on the Eastern Front was often gruelling; more than 30,000 men were killed in the Battle of Tannenberg alone.**

OPPOSITE TOP RIGHT: **Tsar Nicholas II takes command of Russia's war effort. His failure to improve on the performance of his uncle as commander further diminished the Tsar's popularity at home, a factor in provoking the Russian Revolution.**

OPPOSITE MIDDLE INSET: **Map published in the** *Daily Mail* **on 13 November 1914.**

OPPOSITE MIDDLE RIGHT: **Russian soldiers creep across no man's land to cut wires in front of German Trenches. Trench warfare was rare in the east because the front was so long.**

OPPOSITE BOTTOM: **Russian soldiers on training exercises.**

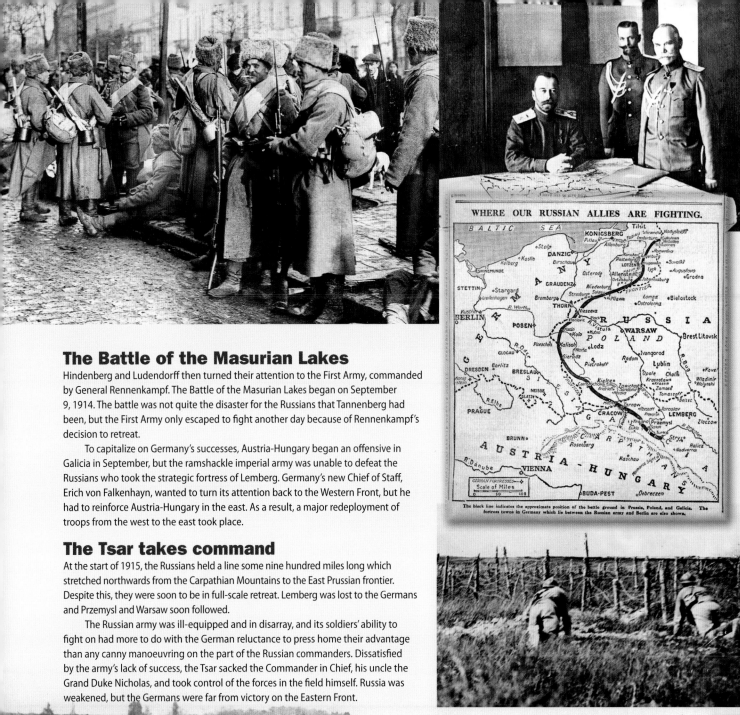

The Battle of the Masurian Lakes

Hindenberg and Ludendorff then turned their attention to the First Army, commanded by General Rennenkampf. The Battle of the Masurian Lakes began on September 9, 1914. The battle was not quite the disaster for the Russians that Tannenberg had been, but the First Army only escaped to fight another day because of Rennenkampf's decision to retreat.

To capitalize on Germany's successes, Austria-Hungary began an offensive in Galicia in September, but the ramshackle imperial army was unable to defeat the Russians who took the strategic fortress of Lemberg. Germany's new Chief of Staff, Erich von Falkenhayn, wanted to turn its attention back to the Western Front, but he had to reinforce Austria-Hungary in the east. As a result, a major redeployment of troops from the west to the east took place.

The Tsar takes command

At the start of 1915, the Russians held a line some nine hundred miles long which stretched northwards from the Carpathian Mountains to the East Prussian frontier. Despite this, they were soon to be in full-scale retreat. Lemberg was lost to the Germans and Przemysl and Warsaw soon followed.

The Russian army was ill-equipped and in disarray, and its soldiers' ability to fight on had more to do with the German reluctance to press home their advantage than any canny manoeuvring on the part of the Russian commanders. Dissatisfied by the army's lack of success, the Tsar sacked the Commander in Chief, his uncle the Grand Duke Nicholas, and took control of the forces in the field himself. Russia was weakened, but the Germans were far from victory on the Eastern Front.

The black line indicates the approximate position of the battle ground in Prussia, Poland, and Galicia. The fortress towns in Germany which lie between the Russian army and Berlin are also shown.

GERMANS BOMBARD THREE ENGLISH TOWNS:

BOMBARDMENT OF SCARBOROUGH.

DAMAGE TO CHURCHES, AN HOTEL, AND PRIVATE HOUSES.

46 PERSONS KILLED AND 66 WOUNDED.

WHITBY & HARTLEPOOL SHELLED.

The war has been brought to our shores in no uncertain manner. At the breakfast hour yesterday German warships vigorously shelled the Hartlepools, Scarborough, and Whitby, the last two being entirely unfortified towns.

Unfortunately there has been loss of life. The names of 10 dead at Scarborough are issued by the police, but there are also some wounded. A considerable proportion of these are after the Germans' own heart—women and children. At West Hartlepool 7 soldiers were killed and 14 wounded, and 22 civilians are among the dead and 50 wounded. The material damage is nearly all to private property. At Scarborough three churches, hotels, and many private houses were wrecked or damaged. Seventeen people were killed. At Whitby, sad to relate, the ruins of the famous old abbey were still further laid low. Two people were killed and two wounded.

The patrol ships engaged the Germans on the spot and a patrolling squadron went in pursuit, but the enemy escaped at full speed in the mist. But the splendid outstanding fact is that England is cool and ready for the enemy.

Admiralty, Wednesday, 11.25 a.m.
German movements of some importance are taking place this morning in the North Sea.

Scarborough and Hartlepool have been shelled and our flotillas have at various points been engaged.

The situation is developing.

War Office, Wednesday, 1.45 p.m.
The Fortress Commander at West Hartlepool reports that German war vessels engaged that fortress between 8 o'clock and 9 o'clock this morning. The enemy were driven off.

A small German war vessel also opened fire on Scarborough and Whitby.

SCENE OF THE GERMAN RAID.

Contour map of the coast from Hartlepool to Scarborough. In the corner is a plan of Scarborough.

ing I was getting up as usual to go to business. The morning was very hazy, and there was a dense fog over the sea. My house is close to the railway station, just on the turning facing the railway. I was on the landing outside my room when I

Daily Mail
THE PAPER THAT PERSISTENTLY FOREWARNED THE PUBLIC ABOUT

DAILY MAIL DECEMBER 17, 1914

Germans bombard three English towns

The war has been brought to our shores in no uncertain manner. At the breakfast hour yesterday German warships vigorously shelled the Hartlepools, Scarborough, and Whitby, the last two being entirely unfortified towns.

Unfortunately there has been loss of life. The names of 17 dead at Scarborough are issued by the police but there are also some wounded. A considerable proportion of these are after the German's own heart – women and children. At West Hartlepool, 7 soldiers were killed and 14 wounded, and 22 civilians are among the dead and 50 wounded. The material damage is nearly all to private property. At Scarborough three churches, hotels, and many private houses were wrecked or damaged. At Whitby, sad to relate, the ruins of the famous old abbey were still further laid low. Two people were killed and two wounded.

The patrol ships engaged the Germans on the spot and a patrolling squadron went in pursuit, but the enemy escaped at full speed in the mist. But the splendid outstanding fact is that England is cool and ready for the enemy.

What was their object?

Yesterday for the first time in two centuries British towns were shelled by a foreign foe and British blood spilt on British soil. What was the German object in attacking unfortified coast resorts and a commercial harbour?

The first motive was to throw a sop to their hatred of England. Held back from Calais, checked in Poland, with Turkey staggering under redoubtable blows, and Austria dismayed, German militarism felt something must be achieved against its most detested foe.

The second motive was to take the revenge the German public has demanded for the annihilation of Admiral von Spee's squadron in the South Atlantic.

The third motive was to proclaim, especially to neutral countries, that German ships could move in the North Sea.

The fourth motive was the vain hope of creating panic so that troops might be kept here who would otherwise be sent to the Continent.

The fifth motive, and the most important, was to force the British Admiralty to keep a larger force than hitherto in the narrower part of the North Sea where that force would be liable to constant mine and submarine attacks from the Germans.

There will be no panic

Neither the British Admiralty nor the British public will fall into the snare. There will be no panic. There is rather a sense of stern content and satisfaction that the issue has at last been made clear. The war has come home to the nation and the nation is ready.

The Germans show no respect for the laws of the war. We must defend our homes against their methods. We must recognize that in this age of mines, submarines, and aircraft the conditions of war have changed. Our Scarboroughs and Hartlepools must have adequate defence. The nation is not taken aback. The German belief that a show of force on the coast or half a dozen bombs from a Zeppelin can demoralise the British people is a pitiful delusion. What the nation realizes from yesterday's events is that new and sterner efforts must be made to win, that more aid must be sent to our Allies, and that the preoccupation of every man and every woman must be to crush for ever the tyranny of German militarism.

OPPOSITE LEFT AND ABOVE: **Damage in Scarborough, England, following a German raid. The German High Seas fleet shelled the British coastline on December 16, 1914, killing more than one hundred civilians.**

OPPOSITE RIGHT ABOVE AND BELOW: **The towns of Hartlepool (above) and Whitby (below) were also struck.**

LEFT: **The historic ruins of Whitby Abbey were hit in the attack.**

DAILY MAIL OCTOBER 16, 1914

The arrival of the Canadians

Plymouth has been the scene of many memorable incidents in British history, but never of a more stirring and significant one than when yesterday the transports bearing the Canadian troops dropped anchor in its harbour. They received a west-country welcome that was local in form but absolutely national in the spirit behind it. What Plymouth was privileged to witness was something more than the arrival of so many thousands of hardy natural soldiers; it was a living picture of the Empire in action; it was the scattering of all the illusions of Imperial disintegration with which the Germans have bemused themselves; it was a spectacle, hardly to be paralleled since the Crusades, of free and self-governing communities voluntarily embracing a cause that passionately appeals to their hearts and consciences.

CHRISTMAS TREES IN GERMAN TRENCHES.

TROOPS FEAST WHILE BELGIANS FAST.

FROM OUR SPECIAL CORRESPONDENT, JAMES DUNN.

ROTTERDAM, Friday.

Sentiment and shrapnel mingled in the German trenches this Christmastide. From correspondents at Sluis, Maastricht, Bergen-op-Zoom, and Sas van Gent I have received reports stating that great Christmas celebrations have taken place in the trenches, at the depots, and along the frontier. The enemy made merry in obedience to the military order, for notices were issued several days ago that the troops must do their best to enjoy Yuletide.

Hundreds of thousands of parcels arrived from Germany containing knitted articles, sweets, cakes, and tobacco. In addition the poor Belgian peasantry were bled to assist the German Christmas. Huge levies of wine and cigars were made in Ghent and Bruges, and the Belgian people were even asked to make Christmas cakes for the German soldiers. The Belgians in reply asked where the flour was to come from as they had eaten nothing but black bread for a long time, and even that was scarce.

While the German soldiers were feasting, drinking, and roaring wine songs the unfortunate Belgians were glad to have a Christmas dinner of half a loaf. Meat or vegetables are unknown, while butter and cheese are rare luxuries.

Not 'over by Christmas'

Many people had believed that the war would be over by Christmas 1914, but this was hugely optimistic. German troops posed next to road signs pointing towards Paris; French troops did the same beside signs indicating the way to Berlin. But even should one of the protagonists succeed in landing a heavy pre-emptive blow against one of the others, it was never going to bring about capitulation – because this was, when it came down to it, a war of alliances.

For example, if the Schlieffen Plan succeeded and France suffered grievously from a German attack, the country was not likely to surrender as long as Britain and Russia stood by its side. As far as the Triple Alliance went, Germany and Austria–Hungary gained strength from the knowledge that they stood together, although Italy was on the sidelines and refused to take up arms with its partners. The alliances which had brought Europe into war in an almost inevitable progression also worked against there being a swift victory for anyone.

On Christmas Day the opposing forces in the advanced western trenches put their enmity to one side and met in no man's land. It was, however, only a temporary respite, for the fighting would continue for another four years.

ABOVE: **On Christmas Eve, British soldiers noticed Christmas lights appearing in the German trenches and the following morning they heard cries of 'Happy Christmas'. The British responded with similar good wishes in German, giving rise to an informal armistice. Slowly both sides emerged from the trenches and met in no man's land to exchange pleasantries and gifts. The ceasefire also gave** both sides a chance to collect and bury their fallen comrades.

OPPOSITE TOP: **Canadian troops being inspected by General Sam Hughes.**

OPPOSITE BOTTOM: **German dead lie in no man's land as pictured from the French trenches. The German trenches (the white line in the middle of the picture) are just yards away.**

HILL 60 BECOMES A SECOND YPRES BATTLE.

SECOND BATTLE OF YPRES.

FRONT EXTENDING ON BOTH WINGS

HILL 60 COUNTER-ATTACKS DEFINITELY FAIL.

GERMAN LOSSES GREATER THAN THOUGHT.

262nd DAY OF THE WAR.

The German attacks on Hill 60 are still being violently pressed, and the engagement is developing into a second battle of Ypres. The fighting is extending on either wing, and the famous ...

RUSH UP HILL 60.

"THE MEN FOLLOWED SPLENDIDLY."

GRAPHIC ACCOUNT.

The Liverpool *Daily Post* to-day publishes the following letter from a Liverpool officer to his father in Liverpool regarding the desperate fighting for Hill 60:—

"I daresay you will have seen something before you get this about our battle for Hill 60, which started on Saturday evening. I have come through it all right, I'm glad to say, and we hold the hill now, which is a very important position, but it cost a lot of life.

"I knew it was coming off but did not see the use of scaring you days before if I was going to be alive and kicking at the end. I'll try and give you a short account of the affair. This hill, quite a small mound, was about one hundred yards in front of our trenches. The engineers had mined the hill.

"At seven on Saturday evening the mines were to be exploded. When the first explosion took place you really can't imagine the awfulness of it. Well, as soon as the last explosion of the mines had taken place the other battalion were to rush up and hold the top of the hill, and as soon ...

LATE WAR NEWS.

FRENCH OFFICIAL.

Paris, Thursday, 11 p.m.

Near Langemarck, to the north of Ypres, the British troops repulsed two attacks. At Hill 60, near Zwarteleen, the German counter-attacks, whose violence seems ...

ALLIES LAND

TURKISH TROOPS AT

ATTACK

FROM OUR OWN

Enos, the po... Turkish frontie... has been bomba... reconnaissance ...

HUGE U.S. EXPORTS

THE STORY THAT

LORD KITCHENER

TEMPORARY SCALE.

The Western Front, 1915

The year of 1915 was a year of dreadful casualties for very little gain on the Western Front. On March 10, the Allies made their first serious attempt to break through the enemy line at the village of Neuve Chapelle. The settlement itself was successfully seized from German hands, although Sir John French's report on the battle was grim (and a foretaste of worse to come): there had been a gain of some three hundred yards on a front just half a mile in length – but it had cost the Allies 12,000 men, either killed, wounded or missing.

The Allied trenches in France and Belgium were largely manned by the French while Kitchener's British recruits were undergoing a rapid programme of military training. The National Register Bill, introduced in Britain in July 1915, required that every man and woman between the ages of 15 and 65 should submit their personal details to the authorities. However, Britain held out against conscription for another year.

Gas attacks at Ypres

With the redeployment of eight divisions to the Eastern Front, the German military used chemical warfare to make up for the shortage of manpower on the Western Front. The Germans first used gas during the Second Battle of Ypres in April 1915. It caused chaos in the Allied line, but the Germans were unable to capitalize because they could not risk exposing their own men to the deadly gas. The use of poison gas in this way was widely felt to be outrageous. Field Marshal Sir John French described its use as 'a cynical and barbarous disregard of the well-known usages of civilized war and a flagrant defiance of the Hague Convention.' But despite its use, by the end of the battle on May 13, the stalemate remained.

Munitions shortage

A dire situation had arisen with the production of munitions in Britain. Severe shortages had been exposed by the Battle of Neuve Chapelle and the Second Battle of Ypres, where demand had far outstripped supply. When this became public knowledge it brought about a political crisis, and the Liberal government was replaced by a coalition in May. Asquith retained the premiership, however, while Lloyd George was moved from his post as Chancellor of the Exchequer to head a new department, the Ministry of Munitions.

ABOVE RIGHT: **With the shortage of shells having such an impact on the battlefield, ever more British factories were converted to munitions production. Most of the workers in this industry were women.**

ABOVE: **In addition to women, workers from across Britain's and France's empires were put to work manufacturing munitions.**

BELOW: **British soldiers first started wearing bowl-shaped steel helmets after the summer of 1915. They offered greater protection when a soldier needed to look out over the top of the trench.**

ABOVE: **Stretcher-bearers transport a Canadian infantryman to safety. Many conscientious objectors volunteered for this dangerous non-combat job where the casualty rate was high. Others served as cooks or labourers. Until 1916 it was not compulsory for conscientious objectors to enrol in the military but following the introduction of conscription they were drafted and were court-martialled if they refused to cooperate.**

OPPOSITE TOP: **The Battle of Neuve Chapelle was the first planned British offensive of the war. Although, they managed to capture the village of Neuve Chapelle itself, the offensive was eventually abandoned after the British registered severe losses.**

OPPOSITE MIDDLE: **The First World War saw poison gas emerge as a weapon of war for the first time. These British Red Cross nurses, working on the front line, were given masks to protect themselves in case of attack.**

OPPOSITE BOTTOM: **British soldiers resting on a mudbank.**

DAILY MAIL JUNE 15, 1915

Our shell shortage – a French opinion

The lack of shells and ammunition, says the Temps to-night, is the principal reason why Great Britain does not defend a larger line in France. The revelation of this shortage has caused some surprise in France.

How is it that a great industrial country like England, whose territory remains inviolate, has been unable to furnish its Army with the munitions which it needs? The fact is that the manufacture of war material, especially field artillery and shells, is a special industry demanding minute and precise attention. Representative English industries such as sheet iron, rails, and locomotives do not require the work of great precision which, on the contrary, is indispensable to most of the important French industries. It was, therefore, more difficult for England to find workmen capable of learning to turn out war material.

But England is tenacious, and every month her sword will weigh more heavily in the balance.

OPPOSITE: British soldiers try to relax in the cramped muddy trenches of the Western Front.

ABOVE: An 18-pound field gun gets stuck in the mud. The summer and autumn of 1917 would be the wettest Flanders had seen in living memory.

RIGHT: Shell holes filled with water could be used for bathing. During the battle many wounded soldiers drowned in such craters.

GERMANS SURE OF VICTORY.

Impressions of a Returned Prisoner.

" German confidence in absolute victory for German arms has not yet been shaken in the slightest degree."

This is the impression received by Lance-Corporal Edward Wells, who has returned after having been a prisoner of war in Germany since August 29.

" When we were travelling to the Dutch frontier from Erfurt," he says, " I saw that there was an abundance of men and war material, and we could see that the fields were all packed with growing corn. In fact scarcely an inch of soil was left uncultivated, grain and vegetables were growing everywhere.

" I am sure the people of this country do not yet half realise what they are up against.

" I had many opportunities to speak English to the guards at the camp. The Germans are satisfied that the Russians are practically finished with and that a month or so will see the end of their resistance.

" They recognise that England is now their strongest opponent and that the war with our country will continue well into next year, when a complete victory for German arms is in their opinion certain.

" ' We are so well organised, you know,' they would say; ' you are not like us. You do not know how to organise.'

" In fact, the one word they constantly harped on was organisation."

War in the air

The First World War witnessed the birth of aviation in warfare. Both sides had to contend with this new front and develop this new technology for use in war. German Zeppelins had bombed Paris at the start of the conflict, and the British had to face an aerial bombardment for the first time on January 19, 1915. Parts of the Norfolk coastline came under attack, and this was followed by raids on the south-east and the North Sea coast over the next few months. There were few fatalities, but they were almost all civilians. The targeted killing of non-combatants in this way added a new dimension to the war, which was termed 'frightfulness' at the time. By employing this new tactic, the Central Powers hoped to damage morale rather than inflict huge casualties.

War in the sea

Germany declared the waters around Britain and Ireland to be a war region in February 1915 and began a blockade of the seas around the British Isles using submarines and mines. However, the war at sea was, for the most part, a stalemate because neither side was keen to engage the other. The Allies feared German U-Boats and the Germans feared British naval superiority. To try to break the deadlock, the Germans announced that commercial shipping would be attacked without any warning. This caused outrage and Winston Churchill, then First Lord of the Admiralty, condemned it as 'open piracy and murder on the high seas' when he spoke in the House of Commons.

Sinking of the *Lusitania*

The threat became reality on May 7, 1915, in a way which had profound ramifications. Over 1,000 people died when the Cunard liner *Lusitania* was sunk a few miles off the Irish coast. A week before, the German embassy in the United States had issued a statement announcing that the *Lusitania* was a potential target, but only a few among the many passengers took the threat seriously enough to cancel their voyage. The loss of 128 American lives generated a strong tide of anti-German feeling in the United States and was the first step towards American involvement in the war. These same feelings of shock and disgust were also widespread in Britain, where anti-German sentiment rose sharply and violently. This change in the public mood led the Royal Family to change its name from the House of Saxe-Coburg to the House of Windsor.

DAILY MAIL   JANUARY 20, 1916

The deadly Fokker

The series of air fights recorded in the British official report late last night - in which two of our machines were lost and five of the enemy's were 'driven down' – shows the vital importance of combating the new German battleplane. The finest flying men in the world, the British, are being out-engined and out-powered by the deadly Fokker.

The French authorities believe that the latest type of Fokker, which is a monoplane (i.e., with a single spread of wings), is fitted with a 200-h.p. Mercedes water-cooled engine. It is probably more powerful than even the latest French Nieuport or Morane. Its immense engine power gives it an extraordinary speed in climbing. The Germans well know the position and the importance of their engine superiority; witness the constant references in their communiques from headquarters since December 16. They – and these communiques, unlike the wireless, rarely lie – record the destruction in air fights of thirteen British machines and two French.

The matter is of the greatest importance not only at the front but also here, for the Fokkers will no doubt come over to drop bombs.

OPPOSITE TOP: **Bomb damage from a Zeppelin raid on Bury St Edmunds, England.**

OPPOSITE MIDDLE: **The sinking of the Kaiser's battleship, *Blücher*, at Dogger Bank in 1915. The crew scrambles along her plates in an attempt to abandon ship.**

OPPOSITE BOTTOM: **The British fleet, viewed from the deck of HMS *Audacious*. This was** the first major British battleship lost in the war when it hit a mine off the coast of Ireland in October 1914.

BELOW: A member of the Royal Air Force poses with the bomb he will drop on German positions.

TOP LEFT: **A German Fokker. The planes were developed by the Dutch engineer Anthony Fokker.**

MIDDLE LEFT: **The aerodrome in Flanders used by the 'Red Baron' Manfred von Richthofen, who was one of Germany's most successful fighter pilots. He was killed in battle in April 1918.**

BOTTOM LEFT: **A German plane brought down by British gunners in Flanders.**

Gallipoli

At the outbreak of war, it had been thought that the Allies' naval strength would turn out to be a vital factor. The first six months of the conflict had shown little evidence of this, but in early 1915 an Anglo–French task force was deployed in the Mediterranean with the aim of changing the situation. The plan was to attack Turkey, which had joined the Central Powers in 1914, through the straits of the Dardanelles – the narrow waterway from the Aegean Sea which led all the way to Constantinople. If the Allies could take Constantinople, then there was every chance that they would be able to win a passage through to their Russian allies.

Accordingly, in February 1915 the forts at the entrance to the Dardanelles were bombarded by a fleet led by Vice-Admiral Sackville Carden. However, progress up the straits was slow and three battleships were lost to mines on March 18. As a result it was decided that the eventual success of the Dardanelles campaign would depend on the deployment of land forces, an obvious decision in the circumstances and one which came as no surprise to the Turks.

The landings

On April 25, 1915 British and French troops, together with soldiers from the Australian and New Zealand Army Corps (ANZAC), landed on the Gallipoli Peninsula. Turkish soldiers had been expecting the landings and were lying in wait behind strong fortifications above the beaches. British and French troops landing at Cape Helles on the tip of the peninsula came under severe fire and barely managed to capture the beach. At the end of the first day their forces were too depleted to mount an advance beyond the beach.

To the north ANZAC troops faced an even worse situation. They landed almost a mile off course and faced an impossible terrain. Trapped between the sea and the surrounding hills, they were lambs to the slaughter.

DAILY MAIL   DECEMBER 14, 1914

The Dardanelles

The Dardanelles (the ancient Hellespont) is a narrow channel separating Europe from Asia and connecting the Sea of Marmara and the Aegean Sea. It is about 40 miles long. The shores at the mouth are about two miles apart, but the waterway then widens considerably, gradually to contract again until it reaches 'the Narrows' eleven miles up, where it is less than a mile wide. There are two sets of defences, one at the mouth and the other at the Narrows. During the war with Italy it was stated that the Turks arranged a minefield below the Narrows.

The passage of the straits was forced by the British squadron under Sir John Duckworth in February 1807, but he repassed them with great loss in March, the castles of Seston and Abydos hurling down stone shot upon the British ships. The British Mediterranean Fleet also unceremoniously steamed through the Hellespont in 1878.

TOP LEFT: **The Anglo-French fleet, consisting mostly of outdated battleships, made slow progress up the straits and fell prey to mobile batteries operated by Turkish forces. It was difficult to launch a counterattack on a moveable target without sending ground troops ashore.**

TOP RIGHT: **Australian troops sailing to Gallipoli. The boats carrying Australian and New Zealander servicemen drifted off course and the men went ashore at the wrong beach.**

ABOVE: **Troops aboard SS *Nile*, prepare to land on the Gallipoli Peninsula.**

OPPOSITE TOP RIGHT: **Marines land at Gallipoli. Capturing the Dardanelles would have offered the Allies a major strategic advantage: the ability to link up with their Russian allies through the Black Sea.**

OPPOSITE TOP LEFT: **A Turkish shell bursts out to sea as British troops take cover. The shells came from a gun nicknamed 'Asiatic Annie' by the men. When Annie ceased firing, the soldiers would dive in and collect the fish killed in the onslaught.**

OPPOSITE MIDDLE: **The men wait around on deck for the Gallipoli campaign to start. At the outset of battle, the Allies had relatively poor intelligence. They did not know the strength of the Turkish army, which was further reinforced during the naval bombardment, and they were also uncertain of the terrain, having taken what they knew from old tourist guides.**

OPPOSITE BOTTOM: **British and French troops come ashore at Cape Helles on the Gallipoli Peninsula.**

Mayfair Works, Vauxhall. | No. 10,458. | LONDON: THURSDAY, JULY 1, 1915.

OUR BIG JOB IN GALLIPOLI.

THE PENINSULA ONE GREAT FORTRESS.

ALLIED TROOPS OUTNUMBERED BY TWO TO ONE.

TO FLATTEN HIM OUT.

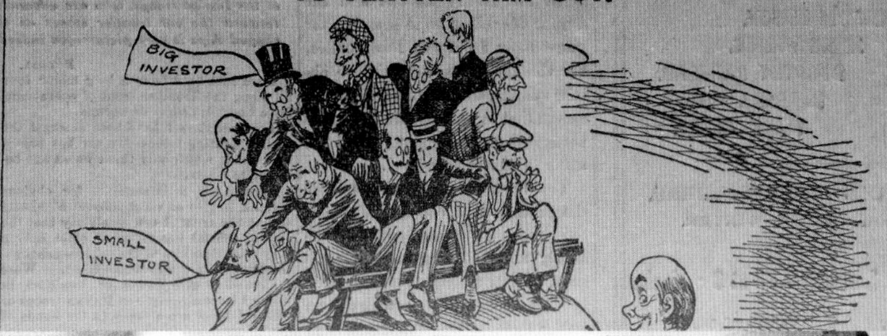

BIG INVESTOR
SMALL INVESTOR

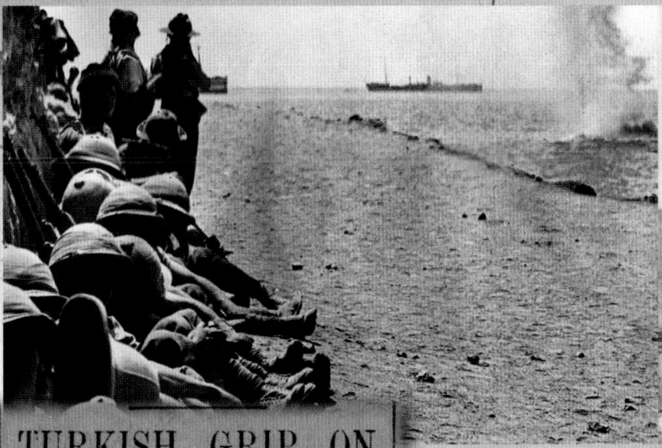

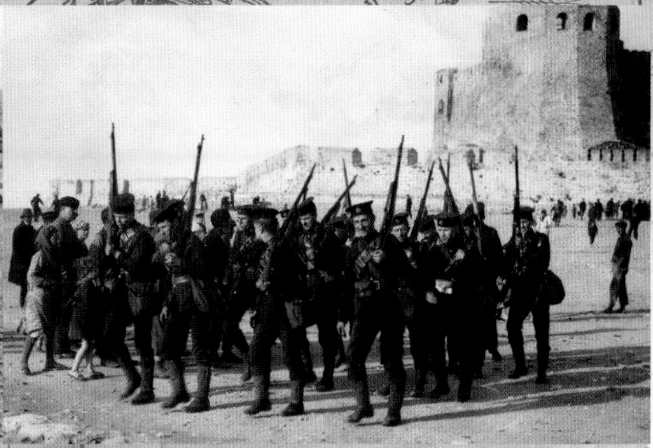

TURKISH GRIP ON GALLIPOLI.

250,000 Well - Entrenched Men With German Officers.

"EVENING NEWS" TELEGRAM.

(From Our Special Correspondent.)

Athens, Tuesday.

The Turks in the Gallipoli Peninsula now have 250,000 men, perfectly entrenched in strong positions, with at least one German officer per unit.

The fighting consists of a series of attacks and counter-attacks. During the day the Allies' attack is assisted by the warships, whose shells search the enemy's positions, inflicting great losses; but at night, when the ships are unable to fire lest they hit our own troops, the Turks counter-attack vigorously in dense mass, after the German system.

Owing to these tactics the Turkish losses are enormous. They are estimated up till the end of last week at 100,000, including many German officers.

The prisoners say that the fire of the warships produces terrible effects, making the Peninsula a sheet of flame.

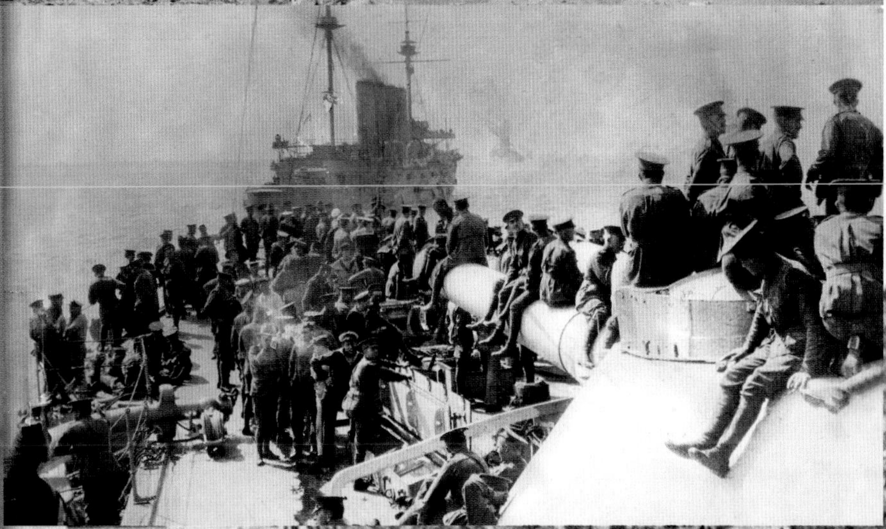

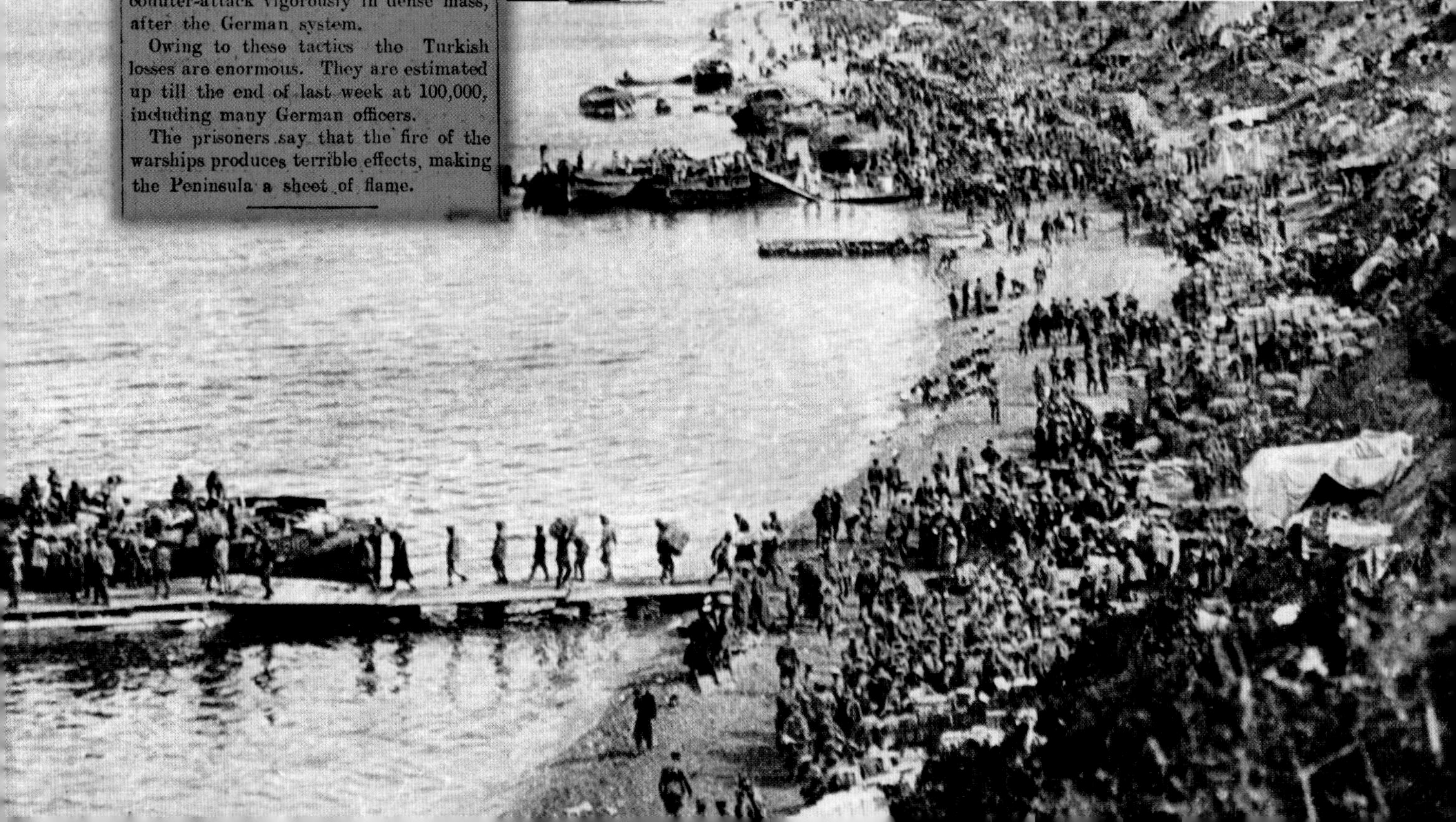

TOP RIGHT: **Members of the Australian Imperial Guards listen to music with the enemy less than 30 yards away.**

BELOW RIGHT: **Allied troops navigate their way along a narrow ridge dubbed 'the valley of death' at Gallipoli.**

BELOW LEFT: **The locals watch with little enthusiasm as marines come ashore. Reinforcements were landed at Suvla Bay in August 1915, but they were unable to have a decisive impact on the campaign.**

BELOW FAR RIGHT: **In May 1915 a truce was declared at Gallipoli for both sides to bury their dead. Many more would die from disease in the coming summer heat.**

BOTTOM: **Going over the top at Gallipoli.**

DAILY MAIL   DECEMBER 21, 1915

Undoing the Dardanelles blunder

The withdrawal of the British troops from two of the three points held on the Gallipoli Peninsula may be taken as a sign that the Government has at last realized the stupendous blunder it committed in venturing upon this expedition, the earlier phases of which Mr. Churchill described as a 'gamble'. A gamble it has proved in the lives of the most heroic of our race. The casualties at the Dardanelles numbered up to November 9 no fewer than 106,000 officers and men. In addition, sickness on this front accounted for 90,000 down to October. A loss of nearly 200,000 men was thus incurred without any adequate result.

Not only did the Government despatch to the Dardanelles forces which, judiciously utilized at other points, might have achieved the greatest results; not only did it divert to the Near East munitions at a time when we were perilously short of high-explosive shells. It also deceived the nation as to the position and prospects after its strokes had signally failed through initial mismanagement or the inadequacy of the army employed. The public has not forgotten the optimistic assurances of Mr. Churchill, Lord Robert Cecil, and Lord Kitchener.

Mr. Lloyd George's speech last evening really contains the gravest indictment that has as yet been drawn against the Government. Here is a confession that when the Germans were in May making 250,000 high-explosive shells a day the British production was only 2,500. Even now he implies that, despite great efforts, we have not equalled the German output. Shall we ever overtake it? Only if the nation works its hardest. The fatal words of the war, he said, were 'too late.' These words have dogged the Allies' every step.

Failure at Gallipoli

The Allies were pinned down but it was hoped that a fresh landing of troops at the parched Suvla Bay in August would bring relief. However, the initiative failed rapidly and Allied casualties, both from enemy action and disease, were dreadful. Churchill, who had been one of the chief advocates of the Dardanelles campaign, had spoken of being just 'a few miles from victory', but by November 1915 it was clear that there were no options left: retreat was the only possibility. Sir Charles Monro replaced Sir Ian Hamilton as regional Commander-in-Chief, and was charged with leading the evacuation. Churchill resigned. The withdrawal from the Straits, at least, was a success. It took place between December and January in almost total secrecy. The entire campaign cost the Allies more than 250,000 men.

TOP: HMS *Cornwallis* fires at Turkish positions in the mountains from Suvla Bay during the Gallipoli campaign. The *Cornwallis* was sunk in a German U-boat attack in the Mediterranean in January 1917.

MIDDLE LEFT: Marines on guard duty at Gallipoli.

**CENTRE: A snapshot of the empty trenches on the Gallipoli Peninsula after the Allied soldiers pulled out. The Allies were careful to disguise the withdrawal from the Turkish army and in doing so made sure that no man was killed during the exit.

MIDDLE RIGHT: Turkish soldiers taken prisoner during the landings at Suvla Bay.

**ABOVE: With such great losses at Gallipoli, these Australian troops made their own crosses. They carved their names and dates of birth alongside the words 'Killed in Action', leaving only the date of death blank.

RIGHT: Map of Sulva Bay which appeared in the January 7, 1916 edition of the *Daily Mail*.

Map of the Anzac-Suvla Bay section, where the heaviest fighting took place.

The Battle of Loos

In autumn 1915 the French commander, Field-Marshal Joseph Joffre, planned an offensive to drive the enemy off French soil. Despite the harsh experience of the spring, Joffre clung to the hope that throwing yet more men and weapons at the German lines might bring about his aim, but his plan failed. However, in the advance in Artois and Champagne British troops did somewhat better. The First Army, commanded by Sir Douglas Haig, took Loos. This time it was the British forces that used gas, despite the adverse weather conditions which meant that some of it drifted into their own trenches. A lack of available reserves prevented the attack from being completely successful and the German forces were able to rally. The British reserves had been too far from the action, and Sir John French was blamed for this error of judgement. In December he was replaced by Field-Marshal Sir Douglas Haig as Commander-in-Chief of the British Expeditionary Force.

TOP: **Britain launched a major offensive to capture the Belgian town of Loos on Sept 25, 1915. The offensive marked the first occasion that the British used poison gas, but the gas was blown back towards the British lines in places, injuring at least 2,500 men. Haig abandoned the offensive after taking 50,000 casualties.**

MIDDLE: **British soldiers returning from front-line duty at the Battle of Loos.**

ABOVE: **Members of the cycling corps mend their bicycles under shellfire. Bicycles proved to be an important line of communication, especially in conditions where motor vehicles were liable to struggle.**

RIGHT: **Sappers, responsible for engineering work, made a crucial contribution to the war effort.**

OPPOSITE TOP: **The Turkish Army marches through Damascus in the Middle East.**

OPPOSITE MIDDLE: **Rollcall in an Allied labour camp. The names** of these Chinese men are inscribed on streamers attached to a rotating drum.

OPPOSITE BOTTOM: **British infantrymen enjoy the modest spoils of war. One is wearing a German greatcoat while another has attached an eagle emblem to his helmet.**

Fighting in the Middle East

As 1915 drew to a close, the Central Powers had the upper hand. Britain experienced a major blow in Mesopotamia, where the nation's interests had become vulnerable when Turkey entered the war. In September a force led by General Charles Townshend took Kut-el-Amara but an attempt to push on to Baghdad proved to be futile and, as at Gallipoli, a bold offensive turned into retreat. Townshend's exhausted troops struggled back to Kut, where they held out for 143 days. The rations were poor – they only had a little flour and horsemeat by the end – and the outcome was inevitable. They finally surrendered in April 1916, and some 13,000 men were taken prisoner by the Turks. However, Turkey's success in preventing the Allies from gaining access to the Black Sea via the Dardanelles (and linking up with the Russian army) was its most significant contribution to the Central Powers' war effort.

BRITISH CAPTURE 1,200

SUCCESS NEAR YPRES.

SUBSTANTIAL BRITISH GAIN.

1,200 YARDS OF FRONT TAKEN.

SUBMARINE COUP IN THE SEA OF MARMORA.

TURKISH BATTLESHIP SUNK BY US.

To our recent submarine successes in sinking the German battleship Pommern, a destroyer of the G 196 class, and also numerous craft in the Sea of Marmora has to be added a capital feat in the same waters yesterday, when a Turkish battleship was sent to the bottom.

AMSTERDAM, Monday.

LATE WA

GERMAN REPU

GREAT ON

21 BATTLE CRUISERS

British soldiers fix their bayonets in preparation for a fresh offensive in 1915.

EXTREME ECONOMY.

A BERLIN EXAMPLE.

NEW MATCHES MADE OUT
OF USED ONES.

The accompanying illustration is a
reproduction in exact size of a match
such as now is being issued in German
cafés, restaurants,
and railway
ishments

COTTON AND DEATH.

TO-MORROW'S MEETING.

Sir Charles Macara will preside over the
great meeting of business men which is to
be held at Queen's Hall to-morrow night
to urge the Government to make cotton
(the basis of all propulsive explosives) contraband.

This meeting is being organised by Man-
chester business men

**GERMAN
DELUSIONS.**

COCKSURENESS GONE
MAD.

DAILY MAIL   MARCH 18, 1915

War work for women

Any woman who by working helps to release a man or to equip a man for fighting does national war service. Every woman should register who is able and willing to take employment.

The object is twofold. In the first place it is an effort to overcome the shortage of labour in many trades. In the second, it is thought that employers engaged in other than government work will be prepared to release from civil service much male labour if women can be found competent to do the work now performed by men of military age and fitness.

Every woman employed will be paid at the ordinary industrial rates. The pay ranges from 32s. a week including overtime in some of the munition factories to 8s. and 10s. a week in agriculture. There is immediate need for women workers in munition and other factories, in offices and shops, as drivers of commercial motor vehicles, as conductors of cars, and above all in agricultural employment. The shortage of workers on the land and in the businesses associated with it runs into many thousands.

The appeal is made to every section of the community. It is recognized that in many instances it will be desirable that women of the same class shall be employed together, and efforts will be made to organize 'pals' battalions' of labour. Endeavour will be made to billet those who elect to assist in agriculture in hostels in suitable centres, and already county people have been approached with a view to making adequate arrangements.

What women can do

'The scheme,' said an official of the Board of Trade, 'has been under consideration for some time, and it is felt that with Lord Kitchener's appeal for "speeding up" in commerce the time is opportune for launching it. If the full fighting power of the nation is to be put forth on the battlefield, the full working power of the nation must be made available to carry on its essential trades at home.

And this is where women who cannot fight in the trenches can do their country's work, for every woman who takes up war service is as surely helping to the final victory as the man who handles a gun in Flanders. With a fortnight's training women can fill thousands of existing vacancies, and also take the places of thousands of men anxious to join the fighting forces but at the moment compelled to keep in civil employment.

Every woman so employed will receive ordinary industrial treatment in the matter of pay from the start, and parents can rest assured that every precaution will be taken to safeguard the welfare of young women employed in factories and elsewhere. Every woman's society, suffrage and otherwise, has been approached, and many have promised their help and the assistance to lay down a hard-and-fast rule as to the trades and employment women can follow, but there are many occupations in which they can be substituted for men.

It is hoped that the first registration of women will be made on Monday. As to the age of those suitable, it is hardly likely that anyone younger than 17 will be needed at the moment, but in the other direction there is hardly a limit. Those who are ready to help the nation should go to the local Labour Exchange and register there.'

TOP: 'Land Girls' freed up British agricultural workers for armed service. They helped maintain domestic food production to sustain the war effort.

MIDDLE: Women pulp paper in Purfleet on the Thames.

ABOVE: Women take over from men in the newspaper printing industry.

Changing roles for women

The First World War brought about a major change in the roles of women in society. Before the outbreak of war few women were in paid employment and most of these worked in domestic service. As men signed up for service, women were required to make up for labour shortages in all sectors of the economy. The shortage of labour became especially acute when conscription was introduced in 1916.

Bulgaria joins Germany and Italy switches sides

The great German advance in the east had provided some astonishing territorial gains: Ukraine, Lithuania, the territory covered by modern-day Poland and parts of Belarus. There was more to come, this time in the Balkans. In the autumn of 1915 Austro–Hungarian forces mounted another assault on Serbia, with German support. This was bad enough for the Serbs, yet another attack from the north-west, but now they also faced another difficulty – a threat from the east. Bulgaria joined the Central Powers in October. Ferdinand, the Bulgarian ruler, had been offered parts of Serbia, a bribe which went down well in a country that had been forced to cede territory to Serbia during the earlier Balkan wars. The addition of Bulgaria was crucial. Anglo–French forces tried to help their Balkan ally by entering Serbia through Greece, but Bulgarian troops blocked their way and Serbia was alone. The Serbian capital of Belgrade was quickly overrun and many Serbs were forced into a full-scale evacuation, travelling through the difficult mountain regions of Montenegro and Albania. Thousands of people died during their flight westwards, towards the Adriatic coast, and the survivors were taken to the island of Corfu in Allied ships.

But despite the considerable successes the Central Powers had enjoyed in 1915 they had not achieved their major aim, which was to force one of the Allied nations to the negotiating table. The Allies had also been bolstered by the addition of Italy, as the former Triple Alliance member switched sides in May 1915. The new year would bring fresh attempts to break the deadlock, and a long-anticipated sea battle between the naval superpowers, Britain and Germany.

TOP RIGHT: **A woman chops down trees for firewood.**

TOP LEFT: **Women form a 24-person-strong fire brigade at a munitions factory in Middlesex, England. Eight of them were on duty at any one time and the day was divided into three eight-hour shifts.**

MIDDLE LEFT: **A Voluntary Aid Detachment Nurse of the Red Cross and the Order of St John tends to a wounded soldier. VADs, as they were known, performed a variety of duties, from assisting in hospitals to driving ambulances.**

ABOVE LEFT: **A woman takes charge of railway signalling in Birmingham.**

RIGHT: **In a scene reminiscent of the Crimean War sixty years earlier, a nurse holds a lamp over a wounded soldier while another feeds the patient from an invalid cup.**

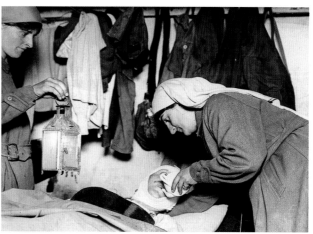

NEW GERMAN ASSAULT WITH 28,000 MEN BEFORE VERDUN.

Verdun

Germany's plan at the beginning of 1916 involved a major fresh assault in the west. Falkenhayn, the German commander, believed that France could be defeated if his men launched an attack at the historic fort city of Verdun on the River Meuse. The general contended the city was so important to France's self-esteem and patriotism that the Allies would invest all their resources in defending it.

The offensive, 'Operation Gericht' (Judgement), was launched on February 21, 1916. Twelve hundred guns – including the huge and notorious 42-centimetre Big Bertha – launched what was to be one of the fiercest bombardments of the entire war.

Within four days the Germans had taken Fort Douaumont which was the largest of the city's famous defensive strongholds.

Pétain takes Command

Falkenhayn's trap was sprung and, as predicted, the French refused to cede a city that was a symbol of national pride, regardless of the fact that it was of no great strategic value. However, the French were not content merely to become cannon fodder for a hopeless cause. Under General Pétain, who assumed command of the city's defences, they determined to fight fire with fire. Pétain, the man who would later be reviled as a Nazi collaborator in World War II, became a national hero for the part he played in helping to save Verdun. Contrary to his later reputation, Pétain was a general of the modern school. He saw that the tradition of noble sacrifice – the traditional French military response – was outdated in the face of modern technology such as tanks and machine guns, and his own artillery began inflicting heavy casualties on the German ranks.

Lines of communication were inevitably badly damaged, but Pétain ensured that one vital road to the south of the city remained open. This became known as the 'Voie Sacrée' or 'Sacred Way' and would be remembered for the ceaseless lines of trucks carrying fresh troops and supplies to the front. They also, of course, brought exhausted and shell-shocked men in the opposite direction for treatment, rest and recuperation. And the losses were heavy; the battle raged fiercely until June.

German redeployment east

As time dragged on there was some wavering among the German hierarchy. This was not surprising; the victory which had been confidently expected to happen within days had failed to materialize after four whole months. Then, with a decision on Verdun in the balance, the news came of a major Russian offensive in the east where General Alexei Brusilov had routed the Austro–Hungarian army. This forced Falkenhayn into a large-scale redeployment of troops eastwards. No sooner had this happened than the British forces began their offensive on the River Somme. The Germans had lost their opportunity and Falkenhayn scaled down the action at Verdun. The net effect was that during the remainder of the year the French regained all the territory they had lost. The combined death toll was about 700,000, with French losses marginally greater. Once more there had been carnage on an unbelievable scale for no discernible benefit. Verdun was proudly declared to be an 'inviolate citadel' defended by men who had 'sowed and watered with their blood the crop which rises today' by the French President, Poincaré. Verdun cost Falkenhayn his job as commander of the German forces, with Hindenburg replacing him as Chief of Staff in August.

DAILY MAIL FEBRUARY 29, 1916

The greatest battle

'The greatest battle of the greatest war' – for so the Germans already describe it – sways to and fro on the hills north of Verdun and seems steadily to extend. The Germans are attacking in enormous force and with the utmost fury. The incomparable French are maintaining the defence with that tenacious coolness and readiness to riposte which distinguish their modern army. There is as yet no sign of any decision and there is a good deal to suggest that the conflict is only in its first stage.

It has been suggested that the Germans are mad in attacking at one of the strongest points of the French line. The German staff, however, has every reason to be anxious to impress neutrals whose decision is believed to hang in the balance by dealing a terrific blow at the French. It has always held that any fortress and any position can be taken provided the necessary sacrifices are made.

The preliminary methods have been the same at Verdun as against the Russians on the Dunajetz – but with this immense difference, that at Verdun the French are well prepared, have numerous lines of defence behind their advanced positions, and are abundantly munitioned. Their most dangerous difficulties are that some new form of attack may be attempted by the enemy, whether by aircraft or by gas. The German bombardment is described as being of a fury which has never been approached before. That gives some measure of its violence. In the culminating point of Mackensen's assault on the Dunajetz 700,000 shells were discharged by the enemy in four hours, while, in addition, many new and devilish devices were employed in the shape of liquid fire, asphyxiating gas, and aircraft dropping asphyxiating bombs. The artillery fire in the present battle, we are told, is changing the very appearance of the country. But the monster guns are not this time all on Germany's side; the French are well equipped with rivals of the monster 17in. Kruppe.

OPPOSITE LEFT: **French poilus manning the trenches.**

OPPOSITE TOP RIGHT: **French troops pictured outside Fort Douaumont on October 26, 1916 after it had just been retaken from the Germans.**

OPPOSITE MIDDLE RIGHT: **French soldiers capture a German dug-out at Verdun. A German infantryman from the 242nd regiment lies dead in the foreground.**

OPPOSITE BOTTOM RIGHT: **Women make munitions at a factory in France.**

FAR LEFT: **Casualties at Verdun. Around 700,000 men lost their lives in the campaign.**

LEFT: **Kaiser Wilhelm and his son meet German troops at the start of the Verdun offensive.**

Jutland

Despite the passage of nearly two years of war, the British and German fleets had managed to avoid any full-scale confrontation. The British navy had more ships and greater firepower, even though Germany had made determined attempts to overtake them in the run-up to war. The mighty Dreadnoughts, with their turbine engines taking them up to a speed of 21 knots, and their 12-inch guns with a ten-mile range, were formidable fighting machines. However, the first Dreadnought had appeared in 1906 and Germany had used the intervening decade to create a response. In addition, Britain's Royal Navy had not been used in battle since the days of Nelson a century earlier, and it was led by the cautious Admiral Sir John Jellicoe.

DAILY MAIL JUNE 3, 1916

Great battle off Danish coast

On the afternoon of Wednesday, May 31, a naval engagement took place off the coast of Jutland (Denmark.) The British ships on which the brunt of the fighting fell were the battle-cruiser fleet, and some cruisers and light cruisers, supported by four fast battleships. Among these the losses were heavy.

The German battle fleet, aided by low visibility, avoided prolonged action with our main forces, and soon after these appeared on the scene the enemy returned to port, though not before receiving severe damage from our battleships.

6 British cruisers sunk

The battle-cruisers Queen Mary, Indefatigable, Invincible, and the cruisers Defence and Black Prince were sunk. The Warrior was disabled, and after being towed for some time had to be abandoned by her crew. It is also known that the destroyers Tipperary, Turbulent, Fortune, Sparrowhawk, and Ardent were lost and six others are not yet accounted for. No British battleships or light cruisers were sunk.

German battleship and battle cruiser blown up

The enemy's losses were serious. At least one battle-cruiser was destroyed, and one severely damaged; one battleship reported sunk by our destroyers during a night attack; two light cruisers were disabled and probably sunk.

The exact number of enemy destroyers disposed of during the action cannot be ascertained with any certainty, but it must have been large.

Scapa Flow

Jellicoe's fleet was based at Scapa Flow in the Orkney Islands, north of the Scottish mainland. Scapa Flow's position gave Britain a natural stranglehold on the North Sea and the German fleet had been confined to harbour for long periods, meaning the Central Powers were being slowly starved of resources. In January 1916 the new commander of Germany's High Seas Fleet, Admiral Reinhard Scheer, came up with a plan to neutralize Britain's naval superiority. He recognized that he had to attack, and formulated a plan to split up the enemy fleet and so increase his chance of victory. The Germans began to carry out raids on Britain's east coast, which forced Jellicoe to deploy a battle-cruiser squadron south from the Orkneys to Rosyth. This was exactly in accord with phase one of Scheer's scheme. His plan's second phase was to lure the battle-cruisers into the open sea by sailing a few German ships off the Norwegian coast. The British battle-cruiser squadron, led by Sir David Beatty, took the bait – and lying in wait for them, not far from the German outriders, was the entire High Seas Fleet. Everything seemed to be proceeding smoothly, but there was one serious flaw in their plans which was completely unknown to the German command. British intelligence had cracked their naval code. Scheer had hoped to overpower Beatty's squadron of battle-cruisers and escape before the main British fleet could reach the scene but, thanks to the code-breakers, Jellicoe was already steaming into action.

BELOW: **The British Fleet pictured shortly before war was declared.**

ABOVE: **The two greatest naval forces in the world in battle in the North Sea off the Danish coast. Although German ships inflicted heavier losses, they also suffered severely and did not risk a second engagement for the duration of the war.**

OPPOSITE: **Men gather on Fleet Street, the heart of London's newspaper industry, to read news of the latest sea battle.**

Battle commences

Beatty's squadron engaged the German fleet at around 4.00 p.m. on May 31, 1916, and both HMS *Indefatigable* and *Queen Mary* exploded and sank within twenty minutes of each other. Out of *Indefatigable's* crew of 1,019 only two men survived, and 1,286 died on the *Queen Mary*. A bewildered Beatty said 'There seems to be something wrong with our bloody ships today.' He was right: later investigation suggested that the way in which the cordite was stored had been at fault.

By now, German guns were having the better of the exchange and Scheer was closing in fast, but he was still unaware of the approaching British Grand Fleet. When Beatty sighted the main body of the German navy he turned his cruisers northwards towards Jellicoe and the main British fleet. It was now his turn to try to lure the enemy into a trap, and they duly followed. When the battle lines were finally drawn up it was Jellicoe who had a huge tactical advantage. By the time the two fleets engaged each other, his ships were arranged broadside across the German line, a manoeuvre known as 'crossing the T'. The Germans were coming under heavy bombardment and, despite the loss of HMS *Invincible* in yet another spectacular explosion, Jellicoe seemed certain of success.

Uncertain victory

In response, Scheer executed a brilliant 180-degree turn, his ships disappearing into the smoke and confusion. Jellicoe was reluctant to follow them, as always aware of the threat posed by torpedo fire, but he soon discovered that he didn't need to. For some reason, Scheer's forces performed another about-face manoeuvre and headed straight towards the British line. Jellicoe was in a dilemma. The Germans now had torpedoes within range – which could cause enormous losses – but engaging the enemy directly could bring an outright victory. He chose discretion and retreated, and by dawn the next morning the German fleet had slipped away. The battle was over.

Germany declared the Battle of Skaggerak, as they called Jutland, to be a great victory. There was some justification in this since Britain's losses were substantially higher. Fourteen British ships had been sunk, while Scheer had lost 11, and over 6,000 British sailors lost their lives while Germany's casualties were fewer than half that. There was certainly some disappointment in Britain, both among the ordinary people and in the government, but Germany never threatened Britain's mastery of the seas again. In fact, Scheer advised the Kaiser that their strategy should now focus on the deployment of U-boats, rather than on using surface ships.

The Somme

The British launched their offensive on the Somme, with France playing a supporting role, in the summer of 1916. An enormous week-long artillery bombardment began; it was a prelude to an attack by front-line soldiers which happened on July 1. Optimism was great among the British troops (as it had been among the Germans in February when they launched their attack on Verdun), and they sang: 'We beat 'em on the Marne, we beat 'em on the Aisne, we gave them hell at Neuve Chapelle and here we are again'. However, the artillery attack had not done its job properly. The Germans were heavily entrenched, and the bombardment proved to be ineffectual. Even worse, it also acted as a warning of the imminent assault. The Allied infantry left their trenches and moved across no man's land, attacking the German positions in close ranks. They were easy prey for the Germans' Maxim machine guns and by nightfall the casualty figure stood at about 57,000 – the worst losses on any one day in British military history. The French had been more tactically astute and made some gains, but overall it was a thoroughly bad day for the Allies.

Haig miscalculates

Field-Marshal Haig, Commander-in-Chief of the British Expeditionary Force, was undeterred by the losses. Although the casualty figures were never so high again, the overall verdict on the Somme offensive was grim. The positions that Haig had hoped to secure on the very first day were still in German hands over four months later, in mid-November. The casualties on the Allied side exceeded 600,000, with German losses almost as bad at up to half a million. British tanks had been deployed for the first time during the Somme campaign but they did not make the impact on the overall outcome that had been hoped for, and by the end of the year a decisive breakthrough on the Western Front remained as elusive as it ever had.

DAILY MAIL JULY 3, 1916

The first day's gains

A great battle had been fought. Another is being fought, and many more have yet to be fought. It will probably be called in England the Battle of Montauban and in France the Battle of the Somme. But, whatever we call it, or however we judge it, we must think of it as a battle of many battles, not to be likened in duration or extent, or perhaps intention, to such affairs as Neuve Chapelle or Loos.

It is and for many days will continue to be siege warfare, in which a small territorial gain may be a great strategical gain; and the price we must pay is to be judged by another measure than miles or furlongs or booty.

We are laying siege not to a place but to the German army –

that great engine which had at last mounted to its final perfection and utter lust of dominion.

In the first battle, which I saw open with incredible artillery fury at 6 o'clock this morning, we have beaten the Germans by greater dash in the infantry and vastly superior weight in munitions. I may, perhaps, claim to be in some position to estimate methods and results. I watched the night bombardments, both German and British. I saw at close quarters the hurricane of the morning bombardment, which heralded that first gay, impetuous, and irresistible leap from the trenches, many of which I had visited earlier, knowing what was to come.

ABOVE: **Men wait for the orders to advance from their reservist trench at the Somme.**

TOP RIGHT: **Soldiers pack tightly into a trench in preparation for an assault during the Somme offensive.**

MIDDLE RIGHT: **The Battle of the Somme saw the first use of tanks by the British Army. Although this new technology did not prove decisive at the Somme, it would help the Allies overcome the deadlock of trench warfare in future battles.**

RIGHT: **South African soldiers distinguished themselves in the battle for Delville Wood, renamed 'Devil's Wood' by the Allies. At the height of the battle, German shells had rained down at a rate of 400 per minute, stripping the landscape bare.**

BELOW: **Members of the Wiltshire Regiment rush on the Leipzig Salient, just south of Thiepval.**

OPPOSITE TOP: **German casualties in a trench taken by the Allies, July 11, 1916.**

OPPOSITE MIDDLE: **Men of the Black Watch eat breakfast on the morning of July 19 ahead of a successful attack on German positions at the Somme.**

OPPOSITE BOTTOM: **The Black Watch pipers play in celebration of the capture of Longueval on July 14, 1916. The village was taken in just twenty-five minutes. The pipers began playing as soon as they realized there would be no immediate German counterattack.**

RIGHT: **June 30, 1916, the calm before the storm.** Two infantrymen share a quiet moment on the eve of the Somme offensive, which was to go down as the worst day in British military history.

ABOVE AND BELOW: **On December 15, 1916, a month after the end of the Somme campaign, the Battle of Verdun also finally came to an end.** Casualties of the two great battles of 1916 amounted to 1.75 million – and still there was deadlock. In both Britain and France there was friction between military and political leaders, the latter determined that 1917 should not see losses on such a scale for so little gain.

HAIG TAKES ANOTHER HALF-MILE OF THE HINDENBURG LINE.

GERMAN TALE OF A SEA FIGHT.

Huns Say We Left Their Men To Their Fate.

FACTS OF THE CASE.

British Destroyer Under Fire
Saved All She Could.

FRENCH LINER LOST.

S.S. Sequana Torpedoed And Sunk In Atlantic.

190 PERSONS MISSING.

With 550 passengers and a crew of 100 aboard, the French liner Sequana has been torpedoed and sunk in the Atlantic.

One hundred and ninety persons are missing. The Sequana, formerly the City of Corinth, was owned by the Sud Atlantique Co. and was

BOMBING THEIR LAIR.

British Airmen Drop Explosives On German Aerodrome.

VERY GOOD SHOOTING.

THE ADMIRALTY, last night:—A squadron of R.N.A.S. machines dropped a large number of bombs on St. Denis Westrem aerodrome this morning.

Very good shooting appeared to

Late London Edition

THE HINDENBURG LINE DAY BY DAY.

British Take Another Half-Mile Beyond Bullecourt.

PLUMER'S

ABOVE: Despite the huge casualties sustained in the early days of the Battle of the Somme, some gains were made by the Allies. Here a Tommy keeps watch in a captured German trench while some of his comrades rest.

RIGHT: The Somme battlefield a week after the offensive was launched. Haig's resolve remained unshaken despite the heavy casualties suffered in those first few days.

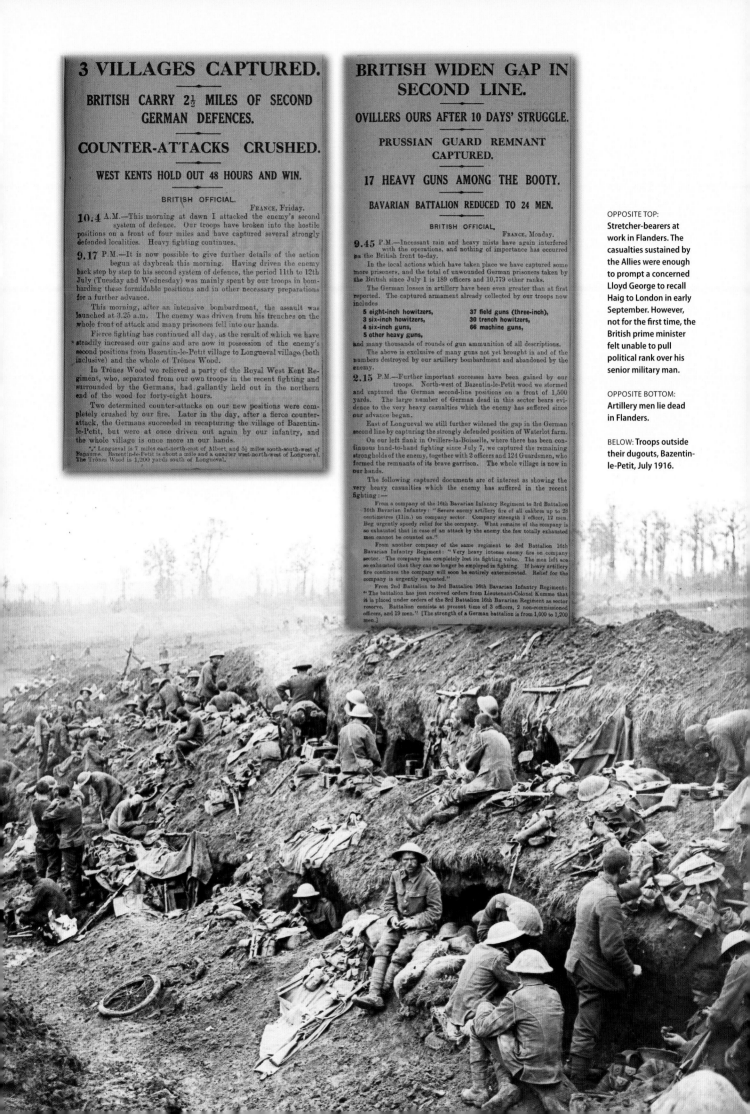

3 VILLAGES CAPTURED.

BRITISH CARRY 2½ MILES OF SECOND GERMAN DEFENCES.

COUNTER-ATTACKS CRUSHED.

WEST KENTS HOLD OUT 48 HOURS AND WIN.

BRITISH OFFICIAL.

FRANCE, Friday.

10.4 A.M.—This morning at dawn I attacked the enemy's second system of defence. Our troops have broken into the hostile positions on a front of four miles and have captured several strongly defended localities. Heavy fighting continues.

9.17 P.M.—It is now possible to give further details of the action begun at daybreak this morning. Having driven the enemy back step by step to his second system of defence, the period 11th to 12th July (Tuesday and Wednesday) was mainly spent by our troops in bombarding these formidable positions and in other necessary preparations for a further advance.

This morning, after an intensive bombardment, the assault was launched at 3.25 a.m. The enemy was driven from his trenches on the whole front of attack and many prisoners fell into our hands.

Fierce fighting has continued all day, as the result of which we have steadily increased our gains and are now in possession of the enemy's second positions from Bazentin-le-Petit village to Longueval village (both inclusive) and the whole of Trônes Wood.

In Trônes Wood we relieved a party of the Royal West Kent Regiment, who, separated from our own troops in the recent fighting and surrounded by the Germans, had gallantly held out in the northern end of the wood for forty-eight hours.

Two determined counter-attacks on our new positions were completely crushed by our fire. Later in the day, after a fierce counter-attack, the Germans succeeded in recapturing the village of Bazentin-le-Petit, but were at once driven out again by our infantry, and the whole village is once more in our hands.

. Longueval is 7 miles east-north-east of Albert, and 5½ miles south-south-west of Bapaume. Bazentin-le-Petit is about a mile and a quarter west-north-west of Longueval. The Trônes Wood is 1,200 yards south of Longueval.

BRITISH WIDEN GAP IN SECOND LINE.

OVILLERS OURS AFTER 10 DAYS' STRUGGLE.

PRUSSIAN GUARD REMNANT CAPTURED.

17 HEAVY GUNS AMONG THE BOOTY.

BAVARIAN BATTALION REDUCED TO 24 MEN.

BRITISH OFFICIAL.

FRANCE, Monday.

9.45 P.M.—Incessant rain and heavy mists have again interfered with the operations, and nothing of importance has occurred on the British front to-day.

In the local actions which have taken place we have captured some more prisoners, and the total of unwounded German prisoners taken by the British since July 1 is 189 officers and 10,779 other ranks.

The German losses in artillery have been even greater than at first reported. The captured armament already collected by our troops now includes:—

5 eight-inch howitzers,	37 field guns (three-inch),
3 six-inch howitzers,	30 trench howitzers,
4 six-inch guns,	66 machine guns,
5 other heavy guns,	

and many thousands of rounds of gun ammunition of all descriptions.

The above is exclusive of many guns not yet brought in and of the numbers destroyed by our artillery bombardment and abandoned by the enemy.

2.15 P.M.—Further important successes have been gained by our troops. North-west of Bazentin-le-Petit wood we stormed and captured the German second-line positions on a front of 1,500 yards. The large number of German dead in this sector bears evidence to the very heavy casualties which the enemy has suffered since our advance began.

East of Longueval we still further widened the gap in the German second line by capturing the strongly defended position of Waterlot farm.

On our left flank in Ovillers-la-Boisselle, where there has been continuous hand-to-hand fighting since July 7, we captured the remaining strongholds of the enemy, together with 2 officers and 124 Guardsmen, who formed the remnants of its brave garrison. The whole village is now in our hands.

The following captured documents are of interest as showing the very heavy casualties which the enemy has suffered in the recent fighting:—

From a company of the 16th Bavarian Infantry Regiment to 3rd Battalion 16th Bavarian Infantry: "Severe enemy artillery fire of all calibres up to 28 centimetres (11in.) on company sector. Company strength 1 officer, 12 men. Beg urgently speedy relief for the company. What remains of the company is so exhausted that in case of an attack by the enemy the few totally exhausted men cannot be counted on."

From another company of the same regiment to 3rd Battalion 16th Bavarian Infantry Regiment: "Very heavy intense enemy fire on company sector. The company has completely lost its fighting value. The men left are so exhausted that they can no longer be employed in fighting. If heavy artillery fire continues the company will soon be entirely exterminated. Relief for the company is urgently requested."

From 2nd Battalion to 3rd Battalion 16th Bavarian Infantry Regiment: "The battalion has just received orders from Lieutenant-Colonel Kumme that it is placed under orders of the 3rd Battalion 16th Bavarian Regiment as sector reserve. Battalion consists at present time of 3 officers, 2 non-commissioned officers, and 19 men." [The strength of a German battalion is from 1,000 to 1,200 men.]

OPPOSITE TOP:
Stretcher-bearers at work in Flanders. The casualties sustained by the Allies were enough to prompt a concerned Lloyd George to recall Haig to London in early September. However, not for the first time, the British prime minister felt unable to pull political rank over his senior military man.

OPPOSITE BOTTOM:
Artillery men lie dead in Flanders.

BELOW: Troops outside their dugouts, Bazentin-le-Petit, July 1916.

Conscription
in Britain

The year of 1916 saw the death of Lord Kitchener, whose recruitment campaign had encouraged more than two million British men to enlist since the outbreak of war. He was aboard HMS *Hampshire* bound for Russia when the ship was sunk off the Orkney Islands. Despite Kitchener's efforts, the rate at which men were volunteering to serve had slowed considerably by the start of 1916 and the British Government responded by introducing the Military Service Bill on January 5. This meant that single men aged between 18 and 41 could be conscripted into the armed forces. Prime Minister Asquith had wanted the sons of widows to be exempted from conscription, but this did not last. The nature of the war – and the extraordinary and appalling losses on the Western Front in particular – meant that married men up to the age of 41 were also being called up before the year was over.

Romania
joins the Allies

In addition to Britain's new conscripts, the ranks were swelled by the addition of a new ally, Romania, in August. It was originally hoped that Romania's decision to join the Entente Powers might tip the balance in their favour in the Balkans – but that hope quickly proved to be groundless. 'The moment has come to liberate our brothers in Transylvania from the Hungarian yoke,' said the Romanian King, but Bucharest fell almost without a struggle on December 5. It looked as though recruiting new allies and new soldiers had made no real difference.

TOP RIGHT: **While en route to Russia for talks, Lord Kitchener (left) was killed when his ship was sunk off the Orkney Islands on June 5, 1916.**

BELOW: **A smokescreen masks an Allied attack at the Somme.**

RIGHT: **8-inch Howitzers deployed in the Fricourt-Mametz Valley, August 1916. The Allies used over 400 heavy guns at the Somme, one for every 60 yards of the front on which the attack took place.**

OPPOSITE TOP: **Wounded men are lifted out of an ambulance wagon at a makeshift hospital station set up in an old farmhouse.**

OPPOSITE MIDDLE: **Reserves move up to support the advance on Morval.**

OPPOSITE BOTTOM: **The barren landscape of the Somme battlefield.**

GREAT SOMME ADVANCE.

BRITISH ADVANCE ON 6-MILE FRONT.

MORVAL & LESBŒUFS CAPTURED.

LARGE NUMBER OF PRISONERS.

SPLENDID FRENCH SUCCESSES.

COMBLES PRACTICALLY ISOLATED.

From GENERAL SIR DOUGLAS HAIG.

FRANCE, Monday.

11.40 P.M.—South of the Ancre our troops attacked to-day and have been everywhere successful. The enemy's positions have been stormed on a front of about 6 miles, between Combles and Martinpuich, to a depth of more than a mile.

The strongly fortified villages of Morval and Lesbœufs (north-west of Morval), together with several lines of trenches, have fallen into our hands.

The village of Morval stands on the heights north of Combles, and with its subterranean quarries, trenches, and wire entanglements consti-

M. VENIZELOS' MOVE.

ONE MORE CHANCE FOR THE KING.

FROM OUR OWN CORRESPONDENT,

ATHENS, Monday, 11.20 a.m.

M. Venizelos (the idol of the Cretans) left the Piræus this morning at four o'clock for Crete, presumably to direct the insurrectionary movement there. The rising has spread ... the island.

Greek Gover ... unfriendlines ...

Colonel M ... left for Salo ... fence army.

M. Venizel ... former Cabin ... (ex-Minister ... and Admiral ... Government ... s.n for believ ... Venizelos wil ... chance.

A telegram ... ri-ting has b ... some Greek o ... the Salonica ...

From ...

A Herakl ... slightly woun ... tered the tow ... from the law co ... been hidden there. The Canea authorities ...

LATE WAR NEWS:

MORE ZEPPELINS LAST NIGHT.

BOMBS ON NORTHERN COUNTIES.

... northern and north midland coun-

'SILK' STOCKINGS.

A BRITISH MARKET CAPTURED.

So great is the import of "silk" and cotton stockings that some of the Leicester hosiery workers are on short time.

Instead of capturing a German trade we are apparently losing part of a British one.

... d cotton ... 3. Of ... 28. Up ... we have ... th, and ... ent us ... pite of ... mously ... Britain, is ... figures ...

1915. ... £262,082 ... £6,699 ...

1915. ... £210,299 ... 1,675,160 ... ER. ... e facts, ... rtunity ... at the ... put by ... Hinck- ... iation, ... of Lei- ... ar the ... else to ... ernment ... th new ... new ... Govern- ... hinery ... the ... merly ... The ...

DAILY MAIL AUGUST 16, 1916

The King on the Somme battlefield

The King returned yesterday from another visit to the front. The following is the General Order to the Army in France which his Majesty sent to General Sir Douglas Haig:-

Officers, N.C.O.s, and men.

It has been a great pleasure and satisfaction to me to be with my Armies during the past week. I have been able to judge for myself of their splendid condition for war and of the spirit of cheerful confidence which animates all ranks, united in loyal co-operation to their Chiefs and to one another.

Since my last visit to the front there has been almost uninterrupted fighting on parts of our line. The offensive recently begun has since been resolutely maintained by day and by night. I have had opportunities of visiting some of the scenes of the later desperate struggles, and of appreciating to a slight extent the demands made upon your courage and physical endurance in order to assail and capture positions prepared during the past two years and stoutly defended to the last.

I have realized not only the splendid work which has been done in immediate touch with the enemy – in the air, under ground, as well as on the ground – but also the vast organizations behind the fighting line, honourable alike to the genius of the initiators and to the heart and hand of the workers. Everywhere there is proof that all, men and women, are playing their part, and I rejoice to think their noble efforts are being heartily seconded by all classes at home.

The happy relations maintained by my Armies and those of our French Allies were equally noticeable between my troops and the inhabitants of the districts in which they are quartered, and from whom they have received a cordial welcome ever since their first arrival in France.

Do not think that I and your fellow countrymen forget the heavy sacrifices which the Armies have made and the bravery and endurance they have displayed during the past two years of bitter conflict. These sacrifices have not been in vain; the arms of the Allies will never be laid down until our cause has triumphed.

I return home more than ever proud of you.

May God guide you to Victory.

George R.I.

THE RIDGE WHICH THE BRITISH HAVE HAD TO CLIMB.

SOUTH.

NORTH.

R Somme — *Suzanne* — *Fricourt* — *Original German front line* — *Contalmaison* — *Montauban* — *Pozieres* — *Bazentin-le-Petit* — *High road to Bapaume* — *High Wood* — *Martinpuich (in hollow)* — *LeSars* — *Warlencourt* — *R. Ancre* — *High road to Bapaume* — *Bapaume*

¼ ½ 1 Miles 2
Vertical scale magnified three times.

The above shows how the British battlefield on the Somme rises. The advance began from south of Fricourt where the "Original German front line" is marked. The top of the hill north of Pozieres has been reached and a footing has been gained in the German third system of defences at High Wood. When our army has reached Martinpuich, another point in the German position to which it is very near, it will have full command of all the ground falling away to Bapaume nearly 5 miles distant, and thus the position of the Germans west of a 12 miles line drawn from Arras to Bapaume will assume the character of an almost peninsular salient.

BOTHMER CAUGHT UP.

RUSSIANS IN CLOSE PURSUIT ALL ALONG HIS LINE.

"STICK-IT" ENGLISH.

GOOD OLD COUNTY TROOPS.

From W. BEACH THOMAS,

FRIGHTFULNESS AT RHEIMS.

BOMBING AND SHELLING.

HOSPITAL DESTROYED.

LORD NORTHCLIFFE AND THE WAR.

A FRENCH APPRECIATION.

FROM OUR OWN CORRESPONDENT.

WOMAN CALLED TO THE ARMY.

FOUR YEARS AS A MAN.

An employer at the Hornsey tribunal appealed for his foreman. The chairman

A MAKESHIFT VOTERS' ROLL.

MR. ASQUITH'S EXCUSE

WAR WORKERS' REGISTER

OPPOSITE AND THIS PAGE: **King George V visited the trenches five times during the course of the war. Here he is pictured at the Somme in August 1916.**

G. R.

Your
King & Country
need another
100,000 Men.

IN the present grave national emergency another 100,000 men are needed at once to rally round the Flag and add to the ranks of our New Armies.

Terms of Service
(Extension of Age Limit).

Age on enlistment 19 to 38. Ex-Soldiers up to 45. Minimum height 5 ft. 4 ins. except for ex-soldiers and those units for which special standards are authorised. Must be medically fit. General Service for the War.

Men enlisting for the duration of the War will be able to claim their discharge, with all convenient speed, at the conclusion of the War.

Pay at Army Rates.

Married men or Widowers with Children will be accepted, and if at the time of enlistment a recruit signs the necessary form, Separation Allowance under Army conditions is issuable at once to the wife and in certain circumstances to other dependents.

Pamphlet with full details from any Post Office.

How to Join.

Men wishing to join should apply in person at any Military Barrack or at any Recruiting Office. The address of the latter can be obtained from Post Offices or Labour Exchanges.

God Save the King.

Unrest on the Home Front

Despite Verdun, the Somme and Jutland, 1916 was to be as indecisive as its predecessor. In addition, war weariness began to set in. By the end of the year each of the main protagonists faced a new and unexpected threat: internal destabilization. The privations of a long-drawn-out conflict meant that the enthusiasm of August 1914 was nothing more than a distant memory. Each country sought to actively encourage unrest within its enemies' borders, while simultaneously stamping on it at home. During 1916 the seeds of revolution were sown; the following year would witness a dramatic harvest which would affect the course of the war.

Britain's greatest crisis came early, at Easter, when members of Sinn Fein took over Dublin's Post Office. Their uprising was brutally put down and its leaders were executed. Meanwhile Britain was trying to encourage revolution in the Ottoman-controlled Middle East. The Arabs of the Hijaz were moved to rise up against the Ottoman Empire and received British promises of independence afterwards. T. E. Lawrence, later known as Lawrence of Arabia, who played a prominent part in the guerrilla war that the Arabs began to wage, knew from the start that Britain had no intention of honouring its pledge.

'Sham' peace proposal

As general disaffection grew, and the strain of the conflict became more and more apparent, the desire for an end to the war naturally gathered momentum. Germany actually sued for peace on December 12, 1916, but the note that was passed to the Allies was somewhat unusually worded, given its aim. It spoke of the 'indestructible strength' of the Central Powers and stated that 'a continuation of the war cannot break their resisting power'. Perhaps not surprisingly, such language did not have the intended effect; not even the most generous of the Entente Powers could see this as being in any way conciliatory. Lloyd George, who had replaced Asquith as Britain's Prime Minister in December 1916, responded accordingly. It was a 'sham proposal', he said, and entering into discussions on the basis of its contents 'would be putting our heads in the noose with the rope end in the hands of the Germans'. Though all sides may have been eager to end hostilities, they were not willing to do so at any price.

TOP RIGHT: A view of the devastation wreaked upon Dompierre-sur-Authie during the Somme offensive.

ABOVE: British soldiers carrying stove pipes during the harsh winter of 1916–17.

RIGHT: The makeshift grave of an unknown British casualty of the Somme offensive at Ginchy. His cap is at the head of the grave and his rifle is fixed to the ground at its foot.

BELOW: A snapshot of death and destruction on the Western Front at Christmas, 1916.

ABOVE LEFT: **British soldiers protect themselves by wearing German body armour picked up off the battlefield.**

LEFT: **Injured veterans of the campaign arrive home in England for treatment in late 1916.**

ABOVE: **Soldiers eat their Christmas dinner in a shell hole at Beaumont Hamel, December 25, 1916. Beaumont Hamel was taken on November 13, one of the final successes before Haig ended the Somme offensive.**

BELOW: **Men of the Royal Warwickshire Regiment take a well-earned rest out in the open during the Somme Campaign.**

German retreat

Withdrawals on the Western Front were central to Germany's new plan. As early as September 1916, work had begun on a new defensive line. It would shorten the front by about 30 miles and, as a consequence, provide a welcome reduction in the demand for resources. The German forces withdrew to the Siegfried Line (or the Hindenburg Line as the Allies called it) in the early months of 1917. A thousand square miles of land, which had been fought over so bitterly and which had cost so many casualties, was conceded almost at a stroke. But the withdrawal was not an unmitigated benefit for the Allies. As they retreated, the Germans adopted a comprehensive scorched-earth policy. The ground which they gave up would have no useful resources left – not even a drop of water, as all available supplies had been poisoned.

LEFT: **The German army left a trail of devastation in their wake. The Allies discover Bapaume ablaze as they enter the town on March 21, 1917.**

ABOVE: **German soldiers left a note in reference to the destruction on Peronne's town hall. It read: 'Don't be angry, just be amazed'.**

BELOW: **Troops from Australia and New Zealand patrol in Bapaume on March 29, 1917.**

TOP LEFT: The French town of Peronne was razed to the ground during the German withdrawal.

ABOVE LEFT: French civilians liberated by the German withdrawal welcome the Allies.

TOP RIGHT: Back on the Home Front, women taxi drivers first appeared on the streets of Birmingham in 1917. While women made inroads into many professions dominated by men, they were still not allowed to drive taxis in London.

ABOVE RIGHT: The devastation in Bapaume as pictured from the town hall on March 30, 1917.

BELOW: German trenches were abandoned following the tactical withdrawal to the Hindenburg Line.

OPPOSITE: Periscopes were used for risk-free observation from entrenched positions.

LEFT: A British soldier keeps watch through a camouflaged periscope. German resistance was ebbing away and, to make matters worse for the German commander Erich Ludendorff, an influenza epidemic broke out so that thousands of his troops were laid low just as the Entente powers were stretching his resources to the limit. Over the next year influenza would claim far more lives than the war itself.

BELOW: Undertaking maintenance work in trenches that were dry, temporarily at least.

Nivelle's spring offensive

The Allies met to plan their own strategy for 1917 long before they became aware of the German withdrawal. This was essentially more of the same: concerted offensives on every front, with the aim of stretching the German forces to the limit. However, such a plan carried with it the prospect of losses as great as those at the Somme – and that possibility haunted Lloyd George, who had become Prime Minister late in 1916. As it happened, a change in France's command structure dramatically changed the Allies' thinking, much to his relief. Joffre was replaced by General Robert Nivelle in December. The new Commander in Chief of the French Army had distinguished himself at both the Battle of the Marne and Verdun. With his reputation riding high, he had little difficulty in bringing the political leaders with him – not least because he told them just what they wanted to hear. His scheme was for a joint Anglo–French spring offensive, on the Aisne. First would come saturation bombardment of the enemy positions, followed by a 'creeping barrage', behind which the infantry would advance. Nivelle predicted that a decisive breakthrough would be made in only a few days. Haig did not agree – and nor did others – but Lloyd George's approval of the plan meant that his hands were effectively tied.

DAILY MAIL FEBRUARY 15, 1917
Sir D. Haig on his plans

'This year will be decisive in this sense: that we shall see the decision of the war on the fields of battle – that is to say, an event from which Germany will emerge beaten by force of arms.'

Speaking in French the purity and fluency of which surprised his visitors, the field-marshal, in answer to questions, said:

As to the next great offensive, it does not matter who makes the first move. If the enemy begins, whether it be in the north or the south, in salients which tempt him or on former battlefields, we are ready to receive him. His temerity will cost him dear. Our armies are well trained and in working order, so that the enemy's defeats will become a rout, depriving him at any moment of the possibility, even far behind his lines, of re-entrenching.

Shall we break through? Without the slightest doubt, with irresistible impulse and in many places. The German defence includes behind the lines a powerful system of railway lines. The first attacks in the great offensive may, therefore, at the beginning be limited. It has taken months and months to hold back this people of more than 50,000,000. It will take several more months yet to annihilate them. But we shall strike terribly and ceaselessly until we have accomplished the total destruction of their armies.

Mutiny in the French ranks

The offensive finally got underway on April 9, 1917, by which time it had already been undermined by Germany's withdrawal to the Hindenburg Line. Nivelle, though, pressed on. The Allies received early encouragement, as the Canadian Corps took Vimy Ridge and the British attacked Arras. But when the main thrust came it proved to be yet another false hope, and the French army sustained over 100,000 casualties in the attack on Champagne. And, not surprisingly, the strict time limit that had been imposed fell by the wayside too. On May 15 Nivelle paid the price for his mistake: he was replaced by General Pétain. Popular though Pétain was, his appointment was not enough to assuage the emotions of the French infantry. After more failed promises and yet more mass slaughter, they had had enough. There was mutiny on a massive scale.

Fortunately, the German Army was unaware of the situation, or they might have seized their chance. Pétain responded to the mutineers with a mixture of carrot and stick: the offensive was cancelled and attempts were made to improve the dire conditions on the front line. Anarchy could not go unpunished, however, and 23 mutineers faced a firing squad 'pour encourager les autres'.

OPPOSITE TOP RIGHT: Canadian troops prepare to go over the top at Vimy Ridge as the Battle of Arras begins.

OPPOSITE MIDDLE RIGHT: A corner of the battlefield at Arras. The British launched the attack on April 9, 1917 as a diversionary operation in advance of Nivelle's main offensive on the Aisne.

OPPOSITE BELOW RIGHT: A battery of 60-pounders in action at Arras.

OPPOSITE BOTTOM: British troops in Arras, June 7, 1917. The offensive cost the British 160,000 lives.

ABOVE: Canadian troops cheer their victory at Vimy Ridge. In a single assault they took the ridge, where so many French soldiers had perished in 1915.

LEFT: The battle-scarred slopes of Vimy Ridge after the offensive.

BELOW: Soldiers pass through the ruins of Athies during the Battle of Arras.

BELOW: **The Battle of Vimy Ridge, April 1917.**
Germans surrender to Canadian forces
during the taking of the ridge.

BEYOND THE VIMY RIDGE.

HARD FIGHTING.

GERMAN LINE TURNED EAST OF ARRAS.

RETIRING TOWARDS DOUAI.

11,000 PRISONERS AND OVER 100 GUNS.

The British Army, continuing its glorious advance, is beyond the Vimy Ridge, so magnificently stormed by the Canadians on Monday, and has turned the German line east of Arras, whence the enemy is retiring towards the Reserve Hindenburg line in front of Douai.

Over 11,000 prisoners and more than 100 guns have now been taken. A feature of the attack was our adoption of the Germans' own liquid fire, which was used with terrible effect.

From FIELD-MARSHAL SIR DOUGLAS HAIG.

Tuesday Morning.

During the night there was severe fighting at the northern end of the VIMY RIDGE [north of Arras], where the enemy had retained a footing. He was ejected, and an attempted counter-attack failed to materialise. The eastern slope of the ridge has been cleared of the enemy and counter-attacks repulsed.

Our troops advanced and seized the village of FAMPOUX [3 miles east of Arras] and neighbouring defences north and south of the [river] SCARPE.

The number of prisoners taken yesterday exceeds 9,000, and over 40 guns have been captured.

In the neighbourhood of ST. QUENTIN the enemy has been driven from the high ground between LE VERGUIER and HARGICOURT [north-west of the town].

Fighting continues throughout the whole battle front.

After an intense bombardment the enemy made a strong attack last night on a narrow front south-east of Ypres and succeeded in reaching our support line. He was immediately ejected from our trenches, leaving several dead.

Tuesday Night.

Our operations have been continued energetically to-day in spite of

HAIG'S GREAT OFFENSIVE.

SPLENDID BRITISH ADVANCE.

VIMY RIDGE CAPTURED.

MANY FORTRESSES STORMED.

OVER 6,000 PRISONERS.

GLORIOUS CANADIAN DASH.

SUCCESSES ALL THE WAY.

The British Army attacked yesterday north and south of Arras and scored the greatest gains of any single day in the war, including the capture of the Vimy Ridge and many other fortresses. Over 6,000 prisoners were taken.

From FIELD-MARSHAL SIR DOUGLAS HAIG.

Monday, 11.25 a.m.

We attacked at 5.30 this morning on a wide front. From south of Arras to south of Lens [9 miles north-north-east of Arras] our troops have everywhere penetrated the enemy's lines, and are making satisfactory progress at all points.

In the direction of Cambrai [south-east of Arras] we have stormed the villages of HERMIES and BOURSIES [8 miles east of Bapaume] and have penetrated into HAVRINCOURT WOOD [south of these two villages].

In the direction of St. Quentin we have captured FRESNOY-LE-PETIT [3 miles north-west of St. Quentin] and have advanced our line south-east of LE VERGUIER [6 miles north-west of St. Quentin].

No estimate of the prisoners taken can yet be given, but considerable numbers are reported to have been captured.

Monday Night.

Operations continue to be carried out successfully in accordance with plan. Our troops have everywhere stormed the enemy's defences from HENIN-SUR-COJEUL [5 miles south-east of Arras] to the southern outskirts of GIVENCHY-EN-GOHELLE [6 miles north of Arras] to a depth of from 2 to 3 miles (on a front of 11 miles), and our advance continues.

The enemy's forward defences on this front, including the VIMY RIDGE [north of Arras], which was carried by Canadian troops, were captured early in the morning.

These defences comprise a network of trenches and the fortified localities NEUVILLE VITASSE [south-east of Arras], TELEGRAPH HILL (........ by north), TILLOY-LEZ-MOF...... [south-east of Arras], OB-...... ST. LAURENT B...... [north-east of Arras], LES ...... FARM ....

STORY OF THE BATTLE.

TANKS IN ACTION.

ARMY'S 'BANK HOLIDAY.'

From W. BEACH THOMAS.

WAR CORRESPONDENTS' HEADQUARTERS, Monday Morning.

At 5.30 this morning Sir Douglas Haig by deliberate choice threw the weight of the British Army against perhaps the strongest force of the enemy ever yet concentrated in such a fortress.

Near Arras our troops leapt to the attack in the midst of such artillery fire as the world has never seen. It was accompanied by an onslaught of strange engines of war, while overhead, as soon as the clouds allowed, our aeroplanes, moving at 130 miles an hour, rushed to tackle any German machines they could find.

I saw all the Somme battle, but never such a scene as this. The shock was beyond all grasp of mind or senses, though I saw it only as panorama from the neighbourhood of the guns and not the trenches.

We attacked in order to wreck the flower of the German Army who fled in fear of rout from the Somme battlefield. Would they or would they not face us here and put it to the touch? Would Rupprecht of Bavaria take the challenge of General Allenby and General Horne, Sir Douglas Haig's chief lieutenants in the battle?

Up to now, at any rate, they had men massed and guns concentrated here; so, too, was their ammunition. One store of it, hit by a 60-pounder shell, had already exploded with such force as to wreck windows well behind our line.

It is useless to try to describe the momentum behind the lines. As we moved up in the darkness past tramping men and bivouacs and the enormous apparatus of war, the flashes reflected from the low clouds lit the road and field continuously, but later the bombardment flickered and wavered, and when I reached the observation point the fireworks were almost normal.

AWFUL SHELLING.

But the hour was near, and when it struck all arrears were made good in an instant. The fitful flashes were concentrated into an ocean of lightning, which broke into one continuous blaze about the ....

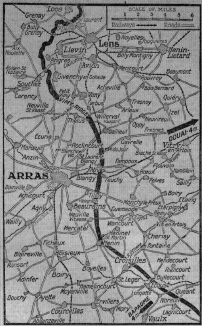

The black line above shows the new British front. From Givenchy, north of the Vimy Ridge, to Henin the line was advanced yesterday from two to three miles. In that section was the heaviest fighting.

when a second storm raised a sort of tidal wave or league-long breaker along two miles of the enemy's coastline of defences. Towards evening a huge progression of smoke, soundless and innocuous, rose and swayed forward, and at one spot behind it a dozen valiant men rushed as if driven by a sudden madness towards the German trenches.

As they returned, successful with the booty they had sought in the raid, a number of our fellows were so excited that they jumped out of the trenches to cheer their triumph. German shells, intermittent and capricious, came whining through the smoke and covered ...... with rubble and worse debris. A...... ...... who had pushed up into ...... to take a picture of the ....

even at this hour was leading out his grey horse to plough a fallow well in front of our heavy guns and in sight of the enemy. The headland of his furrow was a barbed-wire barrier. This was peace in the midst of war. Farther back in a peaceful village I had passed a Scottish soldier in support busy sharpening his bayonet on a grindstone outside a blacksmith's shop.

TANK ASTRIDE A RAILWAY.

FORMIDABLE POSITIONS OVERWHELMED.

Later.

Returning towards the front at noon. I saw everywhere proof that the day had gone from good to better. Prisoners in the common object of the landscape. One ...... division on the north bank of ....

CANADIANS TO THE FORE.

TANKS CARRY A HILL.

GARRISON SURRENDERS.

France, Monday.

The battle which began before daylight this morning on a front extending roughly from opposite Lens to St. Quentin [45 miles] is raging with unabated vigour.

Along most of the front the advance of the infantry was not strenuously opposed and the battle developed strictly in accordance with programme, but near Arras the Germans offered determined resistance and a large pocket of the enemy was reported to be still holding out at midday although entirely surrounded. The famous Harp, a redoubt but little less formidable than the Labyrinth, was captured, with practically a whole battalion.

Several tanks were reported climbing Telegraph Hill at 7.30 this morning, and as this little eminence commands the Harp I think we may reasonably associate the surrender of these ugly brutes with the surrender of the position.

Along the railway running through to the Scarpe Valley [east of Arras] our troops have made good progress, and upon the Lens branch of the line they have gained and taken the Bois de la Maison Blanche.

In Blangy, the suburb of Arras through which the German front line has run since the winter of 1914, several strong points have offered a vigorous resistance, but our bombing parties are gradually reducing these.

I hear that the Canadians have fought their way well forward upon the Vimy slopes, but the resistance here is stiffening.

HEAVY GUN PREPONDERANCE.

One of the most striking features of the great battle is the immense preponderance of heavy artillery which we have over the enemy. It is impossible to believe that anything can live long under such a concentration of guns as we can bring to bear anywhere along the whole front of the offensive. A pretty good proof of this is the thoroughness with which the dense wire defences have been torn and shredded, and it is only when the entanglements dip into gullies so that it is difficult to see them that they have escaped destruction.—Reuter.

GENERALS IN CHARGE.

DISTINGUISHED CAVALRY AND ARTILLERY LEADERS.

Mr. Beach Thomas in his despatch to-day says "General Allenby and General Horne are Sir Douglas Haig's chief lieutenants in the battle.

Lieutenant-General Sir Edmund Henry Hynman Allenby is 56 and a member of an East Anglian family. He served with the Inniskilling Dragoons in Bechuanaland, 1884-5; Zululand, 1888; South Africa, 1899-1902 (despatches twice); was present ...... at Paardeberg; .... relief ...... Royal Irish Lancers ...... 1902 ...... Brigade to 1910; was .... Cavalry.

FIT OR 50?

FLAGRANT EXEMPTION OF YOUNG MEN.

TRIBUNAL SCANDALS.

ANOTHER WELSH LIST.

It is the failure of National Service to provide substitutes for the young fit men required by the Army that is compelling the suggestion to call up men over 41, even up to 50. That failure is shown again and again in the reports of local tribunals.

Our special correspondent in The Daily Mail yesterday said that the men required for the Army are in essential work and cannot be taken till substitutes are provided for them. "The present scheme of National Service should have found these substitutes. It has not done so."

Since March 1 the whole of the military substitution machinery throughout the country has been in the hands of Mr. Neville Chamberlain, who has had full control. Yet for thousands of fit young men, as the reports show, no substitutes are being found.

At the Exeter Appeal Tribunal last week Joseph Honeywill, 25, single, Class A, a slaughterman, had his case adjourned until a substitute could be found. The military representative said that this would never be effected and applied for leave to go to the Central Tribunal, but the Appeal Tribunal refused permission, so that apparently this man is lost to the Army for good.

SUBSTITUTES NEVER TRIED.

The case is typical. Surely it would be better in such cases for the Army to take the man and compel those who are running the business in which he is engaged to take a substitute. Employers place every difficulty in the way of accepting substitutes and appear in some cases to have the power of refusing the substitutes provided.

Before Pembroke Borough Tribunal last week Mrs. Allen, of Pennar Farm, applied for exemption for Reginald Lewis, single, 26, Class A. According to the report of the case in the Pembroke County Guardian, she admitted that she had been offered a substitute, but said she did not try him as he would have been of no service to her. She did not know what the substitute had been before he joined the Army. The military representative naturally asked how she could have known that he would be of no use to her, but the lenient tribunal took no notice and granted six months' exemption ...... of this ...... avoidance that ...... of ...... home and only .... under ......

WILSON DECLARES WAR ON THE KAISER.

R GREAT NEW ALLY.

RESOLUTION IN U.S. CONGRESS.

MUNITIONS AND MONEY FOR US FIRST.

TO RAISE 500,000 ARMY

LSON'S A

tories, bridges, and railways against possible German enemies within their gates. There is a general expectation abroad that within the next few days the Germans will attempt some form of abortive frightfulness designed to "intimidate" the country.

HISTORIC SCENE.

ALLIED AMBASSADORS ON THE FLOOR OF THE HOUSE.

WASHINGTON, Tuesday.

The stage setting for the President's historic speech was most impressive.

the country none dissents from the view that the German Government is the embodiment of a scientific barbarism which must be overthrown if civilisation is to be preserved.

THE GERMAN AMERICANS.

Even the German-American newspapers for the most part express resignation to the fate confronting them. The New Yorker Staatszeitung (State Gazette) says:

The address of the President, demanding full and complete warfare against the German Imperial Government, will come as a shock to millions of Americans of

THE KAISER'S BIG CONFERENCE.

EMPEROR CARL, BETHMANN AND HINDENBURG.

STORY OF AN "OFFER."

The following messages seem to indicate that Austria is pressing the Kaiser to another peace move. There is no sign that the Kaiser yet is ready to put his own hands up.

FROM OUR SPECIAL CORRESPONDENT.

THE HAGUE, Tuesday.

The Berlin Local Advertiser announces this morning that a fresh peace offer will be made on behalf of the Germanic allies shortly. The decision was taken at the last meeting of their representatives. The initiative was taken by Austria.

FRENCH STORM 8 MILES OF FRON

STRONG POSITIONS WRESTED FROM LARGE HUN FORCES.

4 VILLAGES AND SEVERAL HEIGHTS.

FRESH BRITISH GAINS.

The French Army has done it again. Eight miles of strongly organised positions, including 3 villages and several heights, were yesterday wrested from large German forces on the front extending from 2 miles south-west of St. Quentin in a south-easterly direction.

OUR LIGHTNING INFANTRY.

AIRMEN'S ONSLAUGHT ON HUN TROOPS.

From W. BEACH THOMAS, War Correspondents' Headquarters, France, Tuesday.

The United States enters the war

At the start of 1917, Woodrow Wilson, recently elected as US president for a second term, was fighting to keep his country out of the war. He invited the opposing sides to state the terms on which hostilities could end. The Central Powers did not reply, but the Allies' response, issued on January 10, 1917, stated that the aggressors, whose conduct had been 'a constant challenge to humanity and civilization', had to evacuate all the territories that they had invaded and also pay substantial reparations. They reaffirmed their commitment to 'peace on those principles of liberty, justice and inviolable fidelity to international obligations', but Wilson's decision was far from straightforward. Although the Central Powers had violated other nations' sovereign territory, Britain and France were also great imperialist powers. Altruism played no part in Wilson's decision-making, though; he wanted whatever was in America's interests. He also recognized that it might be necessary to commit to war in order to shape the peace in the most favourable way.

RIGHT: The inauguration of President Wilson, the 28th President of the United States, in March 1913. Wilson, a Democrat, was able to defeat the incumbent President Taft because ex-President Roosevelt ran as an independent and split the Republican vote.

ABOVE: Woodrow Wilson had tried to keep his country out of the conflict, but Germany's attempts to incite a war between Mexico and the United States proved a step too far.

OPPOSITE TOP: A meeting of Allies, France's General Balfourier talks to British and Russian officers. Serbian and Japanese officers are visible in the background.

OPPOSITE LEFT: Winston Churchill addresses munitions workers in Glasgow after becoming Minister of Munitions in July 1917.

OPPOSITE BOTTOM: Kaiser Wilhelm pictured with the 26th President of the United States, Theodore Roosevelt in 1910. Roosevelt supported intervention on the side of the Allies in the First World War.

THE U.S. DECLARATION.

I advise that Congress declare that the recent course of the Imperial German Government to be in fact nothing less than war against the Government and people of the United States; that it formally accepts the status of a belligerent which is thus thrust upon it; and that it take immediate steps not only to put the country in a more thorough state of defence but also to exert all its power and to employ its resources to bring the Government of the German Empire to terms and end the war.

The Zimmerman Telegram

Germany launched its tactic of unrestricted submarine warfare on February 1, 1917, but Wilson would still not be drawn in. America severed all diplomatic relations with Germany, but pursued a policy of 'armed neutrality' for the next two months. Three US cargo ships were sunk in March, increasing the pressure. However, the final straw soon came for many people – Germany attempted to exploit Mexico's long-standing grievances against the United States. Arthur Zimmerman, Germany's Foreign Secretary, sent a telegram to Mexico offering support for any action undertaken to reclaim territory lost to the US in the previous century, which included Arizona and Texas. The telegram was intercepted by the Allies and its contents revealed. It had an immediate impact in the United States, and the large numbers of people who had previously been strongly committed to isolationism now became equally in favour of war.

Congress approves military action

On April 2, the President went to Congress to seek approval for a declaration of war; the decision was ratified four days later. The US had thrown in her lot with the Entente but would not sign the Pact of London, the agreement which bound the Allies to act together and ruled out the possibility of concluding separate peace deals. Wilson even studiously avoided using the term 'ally'. In these circumstances, the formal declaration of war on April 6 was more of a psychological turning point than a military one, and it would be some time before the US would be able to make a significant contribution to the armies in the field, something which Germany's high command relied on. Hindenburg and Ludendorff, who were both doubtful about the possibility of victory on the battlefields of the Western Front, put their faith in the war at sea – or rather, in the war beneath the sea. The German U-boats, which were now unrestricted in their choice of targets, could crush Britain while America was still preparing for war. On land all they had to do was play a defensive game.

DAILY MAIL FEBRUARY 2, 1917
Germany defies US

Germany has sent a Note to the United States which in effect declares a hunger war on that country and on the world. A Washington report says that President Wilson may, in reply, warn Germany against unrestricted submarine warfare and threaten a breach in relations if Berlin is unheeding.

The Note announces that German submarines will observe no restraints, and forbids neutral shipping to enter the waters round Great Britain, France and Italy, and the Eastern Mediterranean. It imposes on United States trade these conditions:
1. Only one steamer a week between the United States and Britain.
2. That vessel must run to and from Falmouth.

3. It must be painted in a particular way and lighted at night.
4. The United States Government must guarantee that it carries no contraband, and must warn other ships not to enter the 'barred zone'

All previous promises given by Germany to President Wilson are repudiated. The German demand is a violation of the sovereignty of all neutrals, as the above regulations are not permitted by international law and interfere with neutral rights at sea.

The Note says that the German Government is actuated by 'the highest sense to serve humanity,' and hopes that the people and Government of the United States will 'appreciate the new state of affairs from the right standpoint of impartiality.'

Passchendaele

Following Nivelle's disastrous offensive in spring 1917, the French were in no position to instigate another attack on the Western Front. Haig, however, was determined to do so; his authority had been restored by the failure of Nivelle's offensive, which he had opposed. His idea was to break through the German line at Ypres and then push through to the Belgian coast, severing the enemy's right flank. Such a plan also meant that the Allies would be within striking distance of the German U-boat bases at Ostend and Zeebrugge. All the Entente Powers were still deeply concerned by Germany's U-boat policy and any action which might harm their submarines was therefore a tempting one. Pétain was sceptical, favouring a defensive operation until the US could mobilize in significant numbers, and Lloyd George was still concerned about the possibility of another Somme. But the United States was a long way from being ready, and there were still weaknesses in the French army. Haig saw the chance of Britain gaining a glorious victory. He got his wish and his plans for the third Battle of Ypres – or Passchendaele, as it would come to be known – got under way.

The battle for Messines Ridge

Haig's first target was the Messines Ridge south of Ypres, a key vantage point which the Germans had held for two years. On June 7 General Sir Herbert Plumer led a successful attack on the ridge. From then on preparations for the main assault could continue unobserved and unhindered by targeted enemy action. However, these preparations took six weeks – time which the Germans put to good use.

ABOVE: **British soldiers watch as wounded German prisoners of war are marched to the rear.**

BELOW: **A Belgian woman sells oranges to British troops as they head to the front in Flanders.**

OPPOSITE TOP LEFT: **Canadian medics carry a wounded comrade by stretcher across the muddy fields during the Battle of Passchendaele.**

OPPOSITE TOP RIGHT: **The scene at a field dressing station on the afternoon of June 7, 1917, the first day of the battle for the Messines Ridge.**

OPPOSITE MIDDLE: **Lancers making their way through the ruins of a French village, September 22, 1917.**

OPPOSITE BOTTOM: **The war causes congestion in Fricourt, France, August 8, 1917.**

DEADLY BATTLE FOR PASSCHENDAELE.

PASSCHENDAELE BATTLE.

SEVERE FIGHTING ON SLOPES.

them before, and his men were tuned up to the highest pitch.

Our men on the main ridge rushed on to their first objective line and, after some pause, to their second, using bayonet and bomb all the way, and the distance was a mile. Neither they nor any one else have perhaps ever fought hand-

NEW AIR CHIEF.

OTHER WORK FOR SIR D. HENDERSON.

HUN 'MUTINY' SEQUEL

ADMIRAL CAPELLE SACRIFICED.

TIRPITZ' CAMPAIGN

SIR JOHN SIMON

JOINING THE ARMY IN FRANCE.

Sir John Simon, K.C., M.P., has been

DAILY MAIL JUNE 8, 1917

Haig strikes

We attacked at 3.10 a.m. the German positions on the Messines-Wytschaete Ridge [south of Ypres] on a front of over 9 miles. We have everywhere captured our first objectives, and further progress is reported to be satisfactory along the whole front of attack.

The Battle of Messines Ridge, as the sequel to the Battle of Vimy Ridge, will be almost the greatest battle in our history, if we keep what we have won. At the moment that I write our skied observers see German divisions in mass gathering for attack, but whatever may happen in the future it remains that we took what we meant to take exactly as we meant to take it and at the precise minute we meant to take it.

ABOVE: **A wounded soldier receives a welcome helping hand. The events of 1916 would lead many front-line troops to question the cause they were fighting for, though the camaraderie remained unshakeable.**

TOP: **A soldier takes cover in the flooded trenches of Passchendaele.**

OPPOSITE: **The terrible weather meant that the trenches at Passchendaele often flooded. There were many cases of trench foot, a form of frost-bite, that resulted from prolonged exposure to the cold and damp.**

DAILY MAIL   OCTOBER 17, 1914

Life in the British trenches

Our men have made themselves fairly comfortable in the trenches, in the numerous quarries cut out of the hill-sides, and in the picturesque villages whose steep streets and red-tiled roofs climb the slopes and peep out amid the green and russet of the woods. In the firing line the men sleep and obtain shelter in the dug-outs they have hollowed or 'under-cut' in the sides of the trenches. These refuges are slightly raised above the bottom of the trench, so as to remain dry in wet weather. The floor of the trench is also sloped for purposes of drainage. Some trenches are provided with head cover, the latter, of course, giving protection from the weather as well as from shrapnel balls and splinters of shell.

Considerable ingenuity has been exercised in naming the shelters. Among other favourites are 'The Hotel Cecil', 'The Ritz', 'Hotel Billet-doux', 'Hotel Rue Dormir', etc. On the road barricades, also, are to be found boards bearing the notice: 'This way to the Prussians'.

Obstacles of every kind abound, and at night each side can hear the enemy driving in pickets, for entanglements, digging trous-de-loup, or working forward by sapping. In some places the obstacles constructed by both sides are so close together that some wag has suggested that each should provide working parties to perform this fatiguing duty alternately, since their work is now almost indistinguishable, and serves the same purpose.

The quarries and caves to which allusion has already been made provide ample accommodation for whole battalions, and most comfortable are the shelters which have been constructed in them. The northern slopes of the Aisne Valley are fortunately very steep, and this to a great extent protects us from the enemy's shells, many of which pass harmlessly over our heads to burst in the meadows below, along the river bank. At all points subject to shell fire access to the firing line from behind is provided by communication trenches. These are now so good that it is possible to cross in safety the fire-swept zone to the advanced trenches from the billets in villages, the bivouacs in quarries or the other places where the headquarters of units happen to be.

To those at home the life led by our men and by the inhabitants in this zone would seem strange indeed. All day, and often at night as well, the boom of the guns and the scream of the shells overhead continue. At times, especially in the middle of the day, and after dark, the bombardment slackens; at others it swells into an incessant roar, in which the reports of the different types of gun are merged into one great volume of sound.

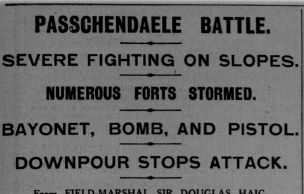

PASSCHENDAELE BATTLE.

SEVERE FIGHTING ON SLOPES.

NUMEROUS FORTS STORMED.

BAYONET, BOMB, AND PISTOL.

DOWNPOUR STOPS ATTACK.

From FIELD-MARSHAL SIR DOUGLAS HAIG.

Friday Night.

Notwithstanding heavy rain which fell during the night our troops succeeded in forming up for the attack which was launched at 5.25 a.m. this morning.

Progress was made along the entire front, which extended from the YPRES-ROULERS railway on the south to our junction with the French on the southern edge of HOUTHULST FOREST [about six miles]. On the whole of this front a large number of defended localities, fortified farms and woods, and concreted strong points were captured by us, together with a number of prisoners.

Fighting was especially severe on the slope of the main ridge west of PASSCHENDAELE and on the main ridge itself south of that village.

Heavy rain again set in during the morning after a brief interval

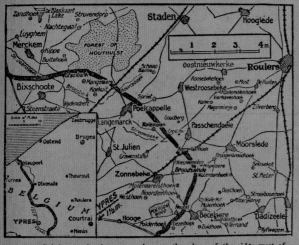

Severe fighting took place yesterday on the slope of the ridge west of Passchendaele and on the ridge south of the village.

Rain and mud at Passchendaele

The rain came earlier than usual and was especially heavy. Haig had planned massive bombardment to signal the start of the main assault on Passchendaele, but the shells broke up muddy ground whose drainage system had collapsed in the deluge. The advancing British soldiers had to contend with thick sticky mud and water-filled craters as well as enemy fire, but the Germans were not in the same position. They had abandoned the idea of trying to keep to entrenched positions in such appalling conditions, and defended their lines with machine guns housed in pillboxes instead.

It took another month before the weather improved and the Allies finally gained a glimpse of Passchendaele Ridge, which had been one of the first-day objectives. The rain returned in October but Haig remained unwavering in his aim. He was convinced that the German army was about to crack and was consumed by the need to capture Passchendaele itself. Passchendaele was eventually taken on November 2, though at enormous cost. The line had only advanced five miles, but more than 250,000 casualties had been sustained for that short distance. Haig's plans were a complete failure. The ports of Zeebrugge and Ostend continued to house the U-boats that had been inflicting terrible losses on Allied shipping, and the German army was far from surrendering.

BELOW: **One regiment marches to the front as another one rests at the roadside on October 14, 1917.**

ABOVE: **Soldiers shelter in the flooded shell holes of the Passchendaele battlefield.**

TOP LEFT: **Wounded men are wheeled through the mud to makeshift hospitals behind the lines.**

MIDDLE LEFT: **Donkeys cart supplies through the muddy fields around Passchendaele on October 31, 1917. The day before, the Germans had repelled an Allied attack with mustard gas.**

BELOW LEFT: **Canadian sappers mark the ground for road construction. All the roads and buildings in Passchendale were destroyed during the battle.**

BOTTOM: **British casualties mounted to almost 250,000 during the battle for Passchendaele. Here the wounded lie in open fields awaiting treatment.**

DAILY MAIL OCTOBER 15, 1917

Swamp of death and pain

Every inch we gained in Friday's battle is worth a mile as common distance is reckoned. Some troops went forward 1,700 yards or even more, fighting all the way; and when their relic came back some part of that heroic journey no enemy dared follow them, so foul and cruel was their track.

They left behind them a Golgotha, a no man's land, a dead man's land. Five or six miles separate our troops from any place where you can step firm, where you can find any break in the swamp. It is a nightmare journey to traverse it, in spite of the ceaseless labour of pioneers.

Our soldiers coming out of this swamp of death and pain maintain incredible serenity. If we could advance so far in such conditions we could go anywhere in fine weather. We were nowhere beaten by the enemy, though more defensive wire was left round shell-holes and pill-boxes and fewer machine gunners knocked out than in any recent attack. We were beaten by the rain that began to fall in torrents at midnight before the attack, so they all say and feel, and so it was.

One of them, still full of humour, said he considered Friday an unlucky day for him. 'You see,' he argued, 'I was first hit in the shoulder by a machine-gun bullet, and as I stumbled was hit in the foot, and as I lay another hit me in the foot and another hit me in the side. Decidedly Friday is an unlucky day.' It was a terrible day for wounded men, and alternate advance and retreat now always leave a wide, indeterminable no man's land from which escape to the mercy of either side is hard. But the best is being done, and the immortal heroism of the stretcher-bearers was backed by both the daring and skilful work of doctors at advance dressing stations and ambulance drivers a little farther back.

The trouble was how to find people or places. Wounded men, runners, contact officers, and even whole platoons had amazing journeys among shells and bullets searching for dressing-station headquarters, objective or what not, and, as we know, even Germans on the pure defensive had similar trouble and their units were inextricably confused. It was all due, as one of them said, to the sump, or morass.

All that can be said of the battle is that we are a little higher up the slope than we were and a little further along the crest road to Passchendaele. How we succeeded in capturing over 700 prisoners is one of the marvels of the day. A marvel, too, is the pile of German machine guns. They are some small concrete proof of the superhuman efforts of our infantry. If the world has supermen they were the men who waded forward up to their hips astride the Ravelbeck and stormed concrete and iron with flesh and blood. They were at least the peers of the men who fought 'upon their stumps' at Chevy Chase.

To-day the artillery fire has died down, the sun is bright, though the cold west wind threatens showers.

The Russian Revolution

The French were not alone in having discontented, dissatisfied and angry troops. There was dissent in the ranks of all the major combatants, provoked largely by hardship and the privations they suffered – and by the impact of mass slaughter for no discernible gain. It seemed as though the consensus between government and people which was required to continue the war was in danger of breaking down, in every nation. All the leaders recognized that the morale of both troops and civilians needed careful monitoring.

In Russia, however, dissent spilled over into full-blown revolution. By the winter of 1916–17 both Russia's army and people were at breaking point. The poorly fed, poorly equipped and badly led troops refused to fight, and the civilian population was faced with soaring prices in the face of dwindling food supplies. Workers in Petrograd – St Petersburg – went on strike on March 8 and took to the streets. In 1905 a similar protest had been quashed with great force, but this time the troops' sympathies lay with the protestors, and the Duma announced that it no longer recognized the Tsar. On March 15, Nicholas II abdicated and a moderate provisional government under Alexander Kerensky was established. This government believed that the war still had to be won and the fighting continued. However, an offensive in Galicia in June 1917 failed badly, leaving the ordinary Russian soldiers believing they were no better off than they had been under the Tsar.

DAILY MAIL NOVEMBER 9, 1917

Lenin overthrows Kerensky

The Petrograd Extremists, with Lenin, the pro-German, in the forefront, announce that they have overthrown Kerensky, that he is in flight, that some half dozen Ministers have been arrested, including Terestchenko, the Foreign Minister, and that their policy is an immediate peace and the land for the people.

They have seized the Winter Palace, after firing several shells at it from a cruiser, and several railway stations, and have issued orders undoing what has been done to try to restore Army discipline.

Petrograd Manifesto

The following, transmitted from Russian wireless stations, is the document announcing Kerensky's overthrow:-

To the army committee of the active army, and to all the workmen's and Soldiers' councils: The garrison and proletariat of Petrograd have deposed the Government of Kerensky, which rose against the revolution and the people. The change was accomplished without bloodshed. The Petrograd Workmen's Council solemnly welcomes the change, and proclaims the authority of the Military Revolutionary Committee until the creation of a Government from the Workmen's Councils. In announcing this to the Army at the front the Revolutionary Committee calls upon the revolutionary soldiers to watch closely the conduct of the men in command. Officers who do not join the accomplished Revolution immediately and openly must be arrested at once as enemies.

The Petrograd Workmen's Council considers as the programme of the new authority:

The offer of an immediate democratic peace.

An immediate handing over of the large proprietorial lands to the peasants.

The handing over of all authority to the Workmen's Councils.

An honest convocation of the Constitutional Assembly.

The Revolutionary Army must not permit uncertain military detachments to leave the front for Petrograd. Use persuasion, but where this fails oppose any such action without mercy. This order must be read immediately to detachments of all arms. To withhold it from the rank and file is equivalent to a great crime against the Revolution and will be punished by all the strength of the Revolutionary law.

Soldiers! For peace, for bread, for land, for the power of the people.

The Military Revolutionary Committee

ANARCHY SPREADING IN RUSSIA.

4th Year of the War: 99th Day.

BALTIC FLEET JOINS LENIN.

REVOLUTIONISTS IN COMMAND AT

A SUPREME COUNCIL OF THE ALLIES.

Establishment of a Permanent Military Committee.

ITALIAN COMMAND CHANGE.

LAST NIGHT'S BANQUET SPEECHES.

MR. BONAR LAW ON THE VALUE OF OPTIMISM.

GERMAN EXCUSES FOR DEFEAT.

Explaining the Retirement on the Aisne Front.

"NO CHRISTMAS CARDS."

A "Too Late" Suggestion as to Economy.

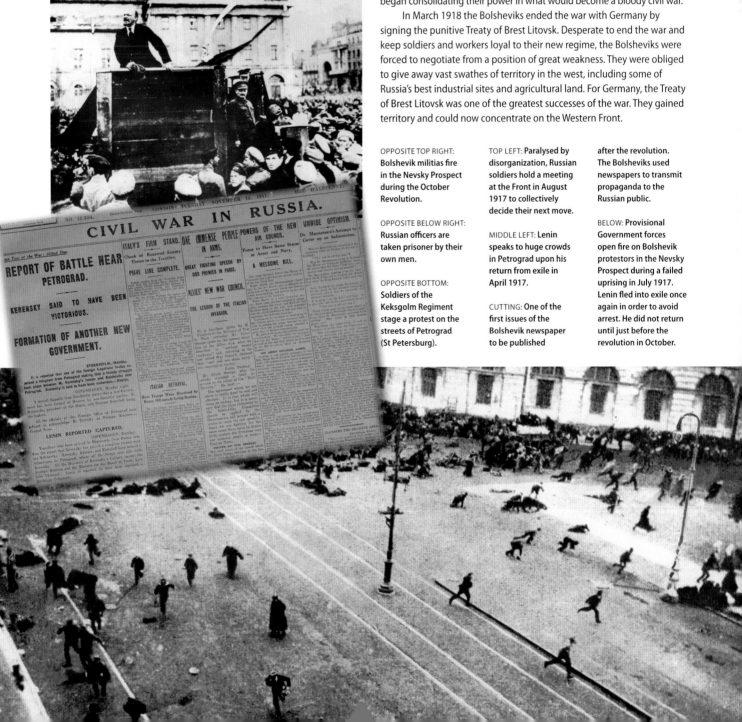

The Bolsheviks seize power

The overthrow of the Tsar presented exiled revolutionaries with the opportunity to return to Russia and take advantage of the situation. One such revolutionary was Vladimir Ilich Lenin, leader of the Bolshevik faction of Russia's Marxist Party. He returned to Russia from exile in Switzerland in April 1917 with the assistance of the Central Powers and called for an immediate end to the war. His message proved popular among soldiers and workers who were deserting in droves and facing severe food shortages. On November 7 – October 25 in Russia, which was still using the old Julian calendar – the Revolution began. In an almost bloodless coup, the Bolsheviks stormed and captured the Winter Palace in Petrograd (St Petersburg), which was being used as the headquarters of the provisional government. With the seat of government in their hands, the Bolsheviks began consolidating their power in what would become a bloody civil war.

In March 1918 the Bolsheviks ended the war with Germany by signing the punitive Treaty of Brest Litovsk. Desperate to end the war and keep soldiers and workers loyal to their new regime, the Bolsheviks were forced to negotiate from a position of great weakness. They were obliged to give away vast swathes of territory in the west, including some of Russia's best industrial sites and agricultural land. For Germany, the Treaty of Brest Litovsk was one of the greatest successes of the war. They gained territory and could now concentrate on the Western Front.

OPPOSITE TOP RIGHT: Bolshevik militias fire in the Nevsky Prospect during the October Revolution.

OPPOSITE BELOW RIGHT: Russian officers are taken prisoner by their own men.

OPPOSITE BOTTOM: Soldiers of the Keksgolm Regiment stage a protest on the streets of Petrograd (St Petersburg).

TOP LEFT: Paralysed by disorganization, Russian soldiers hold a meeting at the Front in August 1917 to collectively decide their next move.

MIDDLE LEFT: Lenin speaks to huge crowds in Petrograd upon his return from exile in April 1917.

CUTTING: One of the first issues of the Bolshevik newspaper to be published

after the revolution. The Bolsheviks used newspapers to transmit propaganda to the Russian public.

BELOW: Provisional Government forces open fire on Bolshevik protestors in the Nevsky Prospect during a failed uprising in July 1917. Lenin fled into exile once again in order to avoid arrest. He did not return until just before the revolution in October.

The Battle of Cambrai

To maintain momentum after Passchendaele, the Allies launched a last offensive for 1917 on the Western Front. At the Battle of Cambrai, which opened on November 20, over 400 tanks were deployed, spearheading the attack. This was the first time tanks had been seen on a battlefield in such numbers. There were some encouraging early gains, but a combination of direct hits and mechanical breakdowns meant that tank numbers were severely reduced after the initial breakthrough. In the end, the German Army counterattacked and the usual stalemate was restored.

Mixed review for the Allies

1917 had been a year fraught with difficulties for the Allies. There was little reason for celebration on the main fronts on land, with a complete collapse in the east following the Russian Revolution, the fiasco of Nivelle's spring offensive and Passchendaele in the west, and defeat at Caporetto in Italy. However, the year ended on a rather brighter note as news came through that Field Marshal Allenby's Egyptian Expeditionary Force had marched into Jerusalem on December 9, capturing Beersheba and Gaza on the way. At sea, the German U-boat war which had been devastating to the Allies in the early months of the year, had moderated somewhat. The Allies had been using a convoy system, with merchant ships travelling together under the protection of warships, and this had helped to improve survival rates. Even so, rationing had to be introduced in Britain at the end of the year, and even the royal family succumbed to it. Germany's attempt to bring Britain to her knees had, ultimately, failed. And 1918 might be much better – there was the prospect of the American Expeditionary Force led by General John Pershing becoming a key part of the effort on the Western Front. Their recruits and conscripts were completing their training and becoming ready for frontline duty.

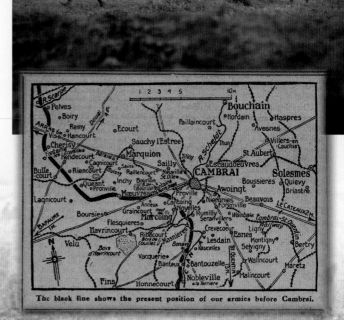

INSET: **Map of Cambrai,** which was published in the *Daily Mail* on November 23, 1917.

The black line shows the present position of our armies before Cambrai.

TOP RIGHT: **Highland** Territorials jump across a German communication trench during an attack on Flesquieres during the Battle of Cambrai.

MIDDLE RIGHT: **British** Infantry dodge machine gun fire near Cambrai. The Allies soon became victims of their own success; the tanks, which had been vital to the spectacular gains on the first day, pushed on too far ahead of the troops, allowing for an easy German counterattack.

BELOW: The East Anglian division occupies a German trench on the first day of the Battle of Cambrai.

quantities owing to the necessary Government restrictions.

NO. 11,243.   Thirty-Seventh Year.   LONDON: FRIDAY, NOVEMBER 23, 1917.   ONE HALFPENNY.

SAUC
Clears up with appeti
"odds & ends," "scrap

ONLY THREE MILES FROM CAMBRAI.

4th Year of the War: 112th Day.

Bouchain

GEORGE MOORE NOVEL IN LIBEL SUIT.

DEFENCE OF THE CITIES OF THE PLAIN.

AMERICA'S FUL
To Declare War
Central Po

TOP: A long ammunition column moves up to the front on November 24, 1917 during the Battle of Cambrai.

ABOVE RIGHT: In December 1917 the troops spend a fourth Christmas at the Front.

ABOVE LEFT: Medics rush to pull a wounded man off the battlefield. Thousands of medical staff lost their lives during the war as they tried to rescue the wounded.

BELOW AND LEFT: The ruins of Cambrai in the aftermath of the battle.

SAVE THE WAR HORSES!

MR. JOHN GALSWORTHY'S APPEAL.

"Honour to the Army Veterinary Corps! As far back as October 16 they had already 'dealt with some 27,000 horses . . . saving the lives of many.' They are a splendid corps doing splendid work. Please help them!" writes Mr. John Galsworthy, the author, in a stirring appeal for contributions to the Royal Society for the Prevention of Cruelty to Animals Fund for Sick and Wounded Horses at the Front, which has the approval of the Army Council.

"Twenty-five horse-drawn ambulances and twenty-five motor-lorries are specially required at once. Now that the situation is more in hand we can surely turn a little to the companions of man. They, poor things, have no option in this business; get no benefit out of it of any kind whatever; know none of the sustaining sentiments of heroism; feel no satisfaction in duty done."

Donations should be sent to Mr. E. G. Fairholme, hon. secretary of the fund, 105, Jermyn-street, S.W.

Time running out for Germany

The German high command had little room for manoeuvre by the end of 1917. It was clear, even to them, that the threat from the U-boats had declined; they could no longer regard their submarines as being an instrument of victory. It was also obvious that the condition of both the German army and the ordinary people – and those of the other Central Powers – meant that the war could not continue for much longer. The Allied blockade, instituted at the outset of the war, which restricted the importation by sea of foodstuffs and raw materials to the Central powers, was continuing to bite, causing suffering, although it failed to starve Germany into submission. However, the troops and people could only be expected to bear such hardships while a great military victory over their enemies remained a distinct possibility. 1918 would bring American forces across the Atlantic in much greater numbers. The German generals knew they would have to play their final cards in France and Belgium, and do so before most of the US forces arrived.

RIGHT: **Pilckem, August 1917. Thousands of horses died on the battlefields of Flanders.**

Operation Michael

1918 started with the German high command having to initiate a redeployment of troops from east to west. A spring offensive around Arras was planned, which was intended to shatter the Allied line and see the German army move relentlessly northeastwards to the Channel coast. This was Operation Michael, and it would rely on a new tactic. Ludendorff decided to put his faith in a rapid infiltration of the enemy line by specially trained 'Sturmtruppen' or storm troops. The Allies were to be given no time to recover, and sheer momentum was to be the key to its success. This was a huge risk, and some senior German officers thought that Operation Michael was far too ambitious, especially given that up to a million men remained on the Eastern Front while Treaty negotiations were still ongoing. However, Ludendorff argued that if he could succeed in driving a wedge between the British and French forces, then victory might yet be possible.

On the other side there was complete contrast; the Allies were in a more defensive frame of mind. There were several reasons for this, and they were partly due to the reverses of 1917. The legacy of Passchendaele meant that Lloyd George felt Haig was too ready to embark on futile offensives, and too willing to play with the lives of his troops. Accordingly, he was wary of committing significant numbers of men into Haig's care. The Entente Powers also realized that time was now on their side.

German successes

By the time the Germans launched Operation Michael on March 21, 1918, only about 300,000 US troops had reached Europe. In stark contrast, trains had been transporting German troops westwards day and night for weeks. This huge logistical undertaking gave some of them an opportunity to desert but, even so, Germany still had a numerical advantage on the Western Front for the first time since the very beginning of the war. The Allies suspected that an attack was imminent but had no idea exactly where or when it would begin.

The start of the offensive was finally announced by a heavy artillery bombardment, including the use of gas shells, during the early hours of March 21. The main point of attack turned out to be between Arras and St Quentin, and the British Third and Fifth Armies bore the brunt of it. The heavy shelling then switched to a creeping barrage as the German infantry began to move forwards. Their initial gains were indeed significant. Succeeding waves of fresh troops joined the attack in a rolling spearhead, a tactic which maintained the forward momentum which was essential to success. The German forces swept across the old Somme battlefield and quickly took Peronne, Bapaume and Albert. The assault threatened to separate the French and British contingents, which could have had catastrophic consequences, and growing disagreement between Haig and Pétain about the Allies' response was an added bonus for the Germans.

DAILY MAIL   MARCH 23, 1918

The greatest battle of all time

This morning the enemy renewed his attacks in great strength along practically the whole battle front. Fierce fighting has taken place in our battle positions and is still continuing.

The enemy has made some progress at certain points. At others his troops have been thrown back by our counter-attacks.

Our losses have inevitably been considerable, but not out of proportion to the magnitude of the battle.

From reports received from all parts of the battle front the enemy's losses continue to be very heavy, and his advance has everywhere been made at a great sacrifice.

Our troops are fighting with the greatest gallantry. When all ranks and all units of every arm have behaved so well it is difficult at this stage of the battle to distinguish instances.

Identifications obtained in the course of the battle show that the enemy's opening attack was delivered by some 40 German divisions [possibly 600,000 men], supported by great numbers of German artillery, reinforced by Austrian batteries. Many other German divisions have since taken part in the fighting, and others are arriving in the battle area.

Further fighting of the most severe nature is anticipated.

OPPOSITE TOP RIGHT: **Conscientious objectors in Dartmoor, England. The caption published with this picture in the** *Daily Mail* **read: 'Working for the Camera – The Dartmoor, "conscientious" objectors are here seen professedly cultivating the soil, but they spend much of their time "on leave" or "strolling on the moors, smoking, reading and talking." Devon people are meeting next Wednesday under the chairmanship of the Mayor of Plymouth to protest'.**

OPPOSITE MIDDLE RIGHT: **Kaiser Wilhelm meets with his top generals Hindenburg and Ludendorff.**

OPPOSITE BOTTOM: **A soldier shields himself as a shell bursts close by during the German offensive.**

OPPOSITE LEFT: **A runner waits for a response to the message he has just delivered. The use of runners was vital for maintaining good communications at the front.**

BELOW: **A Red Cross advanced operating station comes under German artillery fire.**

RIGHT: **Back on the Home Front, two women arrive for their shift on the London underground.**

President Wilson's Fourteen Points

On January 8, 1918 Woodrow Wilson, the US President, delivered an address to Congress. He outlined his ideas for a post-conflict Europe in his 'Fourteen Points' speech, in which he envisioned a Europe made up of nations based on democracy and self-determination, which were armed only as much as was necessary for internal security. A 'League of Nations' would provide collective security and oversee international relations. Wilson did not confer with the Allies before delivering his speech, and not all of it would have been well received had he done so. Complete freedom of navigation on the seas at all times (whether at peace or war), for instance, was a stipulation which would not have pleased Britain, a great naval power. In addition, Wilson's call for transparent pacts between governments was far removed from the secret deals by which many of the minor combatants had been persuaded to support one side or the other. But President Wilson knew that he held a strong hand in January 1918, and he was determined to be the prime mover in shaping the new world order.

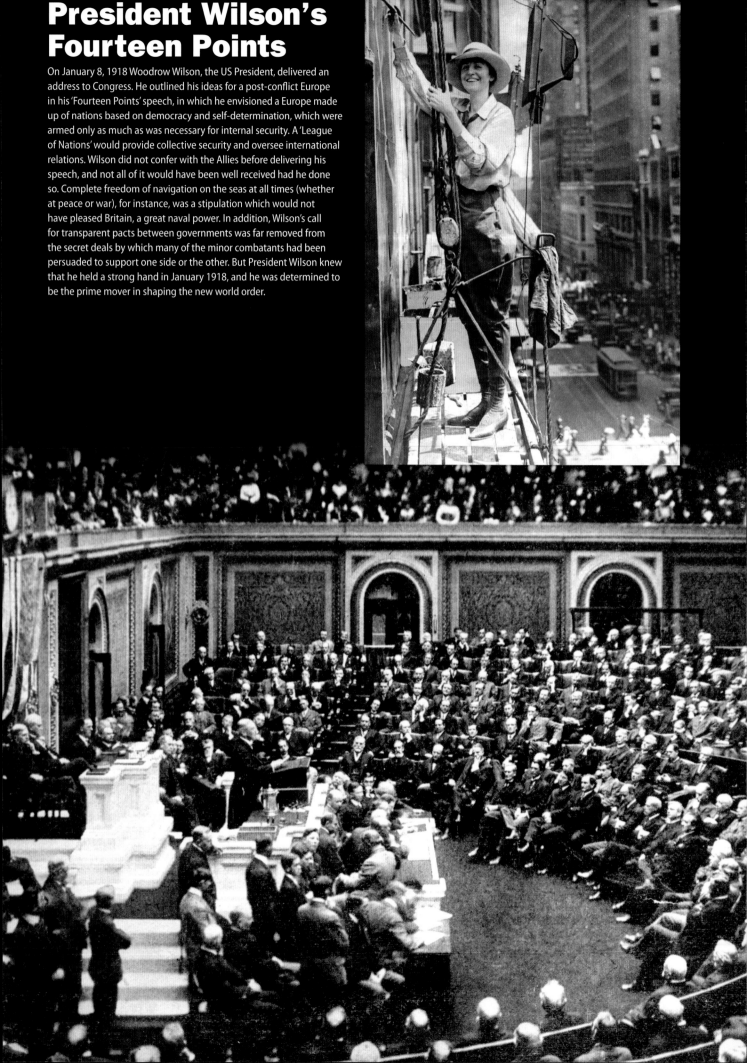

Britain grows weary

In Britain the situation had become delicate. Over six million working days were lost to strikes in 1918, an indication that the government's exhortations to show restraint and support for the war were finally wearing thin. And as insurance against future manpower needs, the 1918 Military Service Bill raised the age at which men were liable to be conscripted from 41 to 50. The Defence of the Realm Act was amended in March to make it an offence for women to pass on sexually transmitted diseases to servicemen, the incidence of which was reaching epidemic proportions, and offenders were threatened with a heavy fine or imprisonment. This was not especially connected to public morality; it had much more to do with the need to have men fit for active duty.

It wasn't just the American soldiers who were eagerly awaited. The war had left Britain close to bankruptcy. By 1918, 75 per cent of the country's national income was directed at the war effort; the nation's resources had never been so overwhelmingly devoted to a single aim. In the end, the final bill would be £10 billion, of which some £7 billion was borrowed. It meant that the financial backing of the US would be every bit as welcome as its manpower and machinery.

OPPOSITE MAIN IMAGE: **President Wilson delivers his Fourteen Points to Congress.**

OPPOSITE TOP: **Artist Lucille Patterson takes on the job of painting billboards on 42nd Street in New York in order to release men to join the army.**

BELOW: **The USS** *Michigan* **transports American troops to Europe. It spent the remainder of the war being used for training exercises in US waters.**

TOP LEFT: **American sailors watch the Changing of the Guard ceremony at Buckingham Palace soon after arriving in London.**

LEFT: **The first female naval recruit in the United States, Loretta Walsh, is sworn in as 'chief yeoman' to do clerical work for the navy.**

Ludendorff's offensives

Marshal Ferdinand Foch became the de facto Supreme Allied Commander of the Western Front on March 26, 1918. He had the immediate problem of pulling together the Allied defences and stopping the potentially disastrous German advance. The town of Amiens, Foch quickly realized, would be an immediate target for the enemy and he decided that it must be defended at all costs. In this he was helped, paradoxically, by the Germans and specifically by Ludendorff, who decided to advance on a wide front instead of concentrating his efforts on taking Amiens itself. As the days passed, the Allied line grew much stronger and better reinforced, while the German line was becoming overstretched and weaker. The German advance finally petered out on April 8. It had lost its vital momentum.

Ludendorff decided to change the point of attack in the hope of revitalizing the attack. A fresh offensive was launched around the River Lys to the north, which had originally been considered as an alternative to Operation Michael. It now became the focus of a secondary onslaught, and once again there was an immediate breakthrough which offered encouragement to the Germans. Haig issued a Special Order of the Day on April 11. This was, in effect, a rallying call to all the ranks: 'There is no other course open to us but to fight it out. Every position must be held to the last man; there must be no retirement.'

Romania surrenders

By the end of April the latest German offensive had fizzled out too. Ludendorff was now caught between the need to make a decisive breakthrough and the necessity of trying to conserve his resources, which were rapidly diminishing. Romania signed the Treaty of Bucharest on May 7, and now posed no threat to Germany; a glimmer of hope. Romania had felt dangerously isolated after Russia's withdrawal from the war and saw the need for an early armistice. Germany exacted a heavy price from the defeated country but it made little difference; the war was now in its final phase.

TOP RIGHT: **Soldiers barricade themselves amongst the rubble during street fighting in Bailleul.**

RIGHT: **A soldier watches an explosion at a munitions dump during a tactical withdrawal on the Western Front.**

BELOW: **British troops retreat from General Ludendorff's latest offensive on April 3, 1918.**

Germans within striking distance of Paris

The final stages had to be played out on the Western Front. Ludendorff tried yet another initiative on May 27, this time against the French Sixth Army along the Chemin des Dames. The German army swept across the Aisne and reached the Marne. This suddenly threatened Paris, which was only some 50 miles away, and there was a partial evacuation of the city. Paris did come under fire from the German guns, but the attack was halted. The German army had made great territorial gains and inflicted considerable losses on the Allies in three short months of concerted effort. However, more and more American divisions were arriving, and the Allied losses were not as critical as those sustained by Ludendorff. In a single month – June – his army suffered over 200,000 casualties. June also saw the arrival of the flu epidemic in the German ranks, diminishing their strength even further.

On July 15, Ludendorff made a final effort to achieve a breakthrough. There was an offensive around Rheims. Three days later the French, who were supported by fresh American troops, counter-attacked. This became known as the Second Battle of the Marne, and proved to be the turning point. From this time on, right until the end of hostilities in November, Germany would be on the retreat.

BELOW: **Wounded British troops at an advanced dressing station following a German attack. Injured soldiers are put on stretchers in preparation for transport to regular hospitals further behind the lines. German prisoners are put to use as stretcher bearers.**

ABOVE: **A labour battalion builds a road through captured British territory on the Western Front. Many of the members of these battalions were veterans who went to France to help with the war effort in any way they could.**

DAILY MAIL APRIL 14, 1918

The line holds but the crisis is not past

The British Army has made its valiant answer to Sir Douglas Haig's general order calling upon it to stand and fight – to the last man - for 'the safety of our homes and the freedom of mankind.'

For the past 48 hours, in the face of repeated attacks by masses of Germans and of a terrific bombardment, our devoted lads have held their ground firmly and unflinchingly. The line is still unbroken, and though the crisis is not yet by any means over, there is at least good hope that the men of 1918 will hold fast and win through like the heroes of 1914. There must still be considerable danger so long as there are signs of a powerful German concentration in another quarter, between Arras and Albert. But each hour gained in the north is of priceless importance.

During the last two days our troops have beaten off an attack at Festubert. They have held Bailleul, a point of supreme importance, as it threatens the communications of Ypres. They have recovered Neuve Eglise, on the flank of the Ypres defences, and they have kept it against repeated attacks. They have maintained their positions on the high ground. They still have the enemy below them in the intricate marsh and meadow land, where movement is not facilitated by the nature of the ground.

Insist on having Condy's Fluid.
CONDY'S FLUID CO., Goswell Road, London
NO. 11,357.
THIRTY-SEVENTH YEAR.
LONDON: M

ENEMY SHELLING

4th Year of the War: 248th Day.

GUNS MORE ACTIVE AGAINST
BRITISH AND FRENCH.

HAIG REPORTS SLIGHT ADVANCE EAST OF AMIENS.

GAS BOMBARDMENT NEAR LENS.

THE WHOLE FRONT.

ALIENS AND MAN POWER.

The Position in Leading West End Hotels.

Men under 51 are anxiously awaiting the statement which the Prime Minister will make to-morrow on Man Power.

In all the heavy correspondence received by *The Evening News* on the subject there is not a single objection to the proposal when applied with justice to every man whatever his nationality, living in the United Kingdom.

The one common demand that with every facility however it equal elements and to demand a man and to to the man who make the provision of the provision of the who make his

GREAT RED CROSS SALE OPENED TO-DAY.

3,000 PATRIOTIC DONORS.

To-day saw the opening of the great sale at Christie's in aid of the British Red Cross Society and the Order of the Hospital of St. John of Jerusalem in England.

The fourth sale of the kind in the famous rooms in King-street, St. James's, since the war began, it is confidently hoped that the remarkable collection of pictures, china, japanese and brought together will be the

KAISER SEES MYST

Yesterday's Casualties in Fowls.

AMSTERDA

Herr Karl Rosner, the w correspondent, writing in th *ger*, says: On March 23 the ted the giant gun which i Paris. It looks more like grey crane than a real gun, distance of 130 kilometres. it fired a shorter distance t the projectile took exactly reach its objective, namely

According to the designer of the long ran Herr Fritz Rausenber Krupp

ABOVE: **Soldiers of the Worcester Regiment doff their caps to the cameraman as they head to the frontline.**

NEW GERMAN THRUST FOR AMIENS.

War: 264th Day. -34th Day of Great Battle.

TTLE OPENED TO-DAY.

TTACKS IN PROGRESS IN SOMME AREA.

T FROM ALBERT TO JUNCTION WITH FRENCH.

G.H.Q., Wednesday, 11.5 a.m.

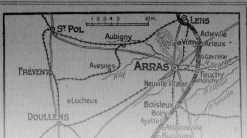

BRITISH HAVOC AT ZEEBRUGGE.

GERMAN GUNS TURNED ON MOLE GARRISON.

No Place of Military Importance Left.

(FROM OUR SPECIAL CORRESPONDENT.)

I have just learned the story of the storming of Zeebrugge, the destruction of the enemy's guns, and the blockading of the harbour.

It is one of the grandest stories of daring in the annals of the Navy.

DESTROYER CUT IN TWO.

Attacking Parties Board Ships and Kill Crews.

A SOUTH-EAST PORT, Wednesday.

A large number of survivors from the special battalion of the Royal Marines who took part in the naval raid arrived here yesterday, and had a rousing reception from the inhabitants.

The first batch arrived unexpectedly shortly before noon, and a number arrived later. One could see at a glance they had

HOLLAND'S

What Allies Will Do Hun T

According to the I situation of Holland pessimistically.

It appears that stands by her claims and gravel via the B

The Dutch Govern requires permission to proceed to Belgium areas, in order to in tracted, the use of th Germany, however Commission to enter there is the question Holland would certa

The Amiens offensive

The Allies were now forcing Ludendorff's army backwards relentlessly. The morale of the rival forces changed accordingly – and the poor situation of the German forces did not improve. The Battle of Amiens took place on August 8, with General Rawlinson leading a combined Allied force. They caught the Germans completely off guard and quickly shattered any remaining hopes of victory which they might have had. Over 2,000 guns bombarded the German line and some 400 tanks were deployed to support the Allied infantry as they advanced.

Allied air supremacy

The Allies now had massive air supremacy, partly due to the RAF, which had recently been formed. Reconnaissance aircraft had improved, and information about enemy positions and batteries could now be relayed much more efficiently. The backroom staff had also finally come up with a solution to the problem of synchronizing machine-gun fire with the rotation of the propellers, some three years after Anthony Fokker had achieved the same thing for the Germans. The rate of attrition among the flyers was high, however: on the first day of the Amiens offensive the RAF lost 45 planes to anti-aircraft fire. Despite this, their contribution to the Allies' ultimate success was significant.

The Amiens offensive was undoubtedly disastrous for the Central Powers, and Ludendorff declared it to be 'the black day of the German army'. The final blow would be for the Allies to breach the German Siegfried Line, and this finally happened on September 29. Even before that, both Ludendorff and the Kaiser knew that the outcome was now set. The only thing left was to bring the war to an end.

WALKING WOUNDED

BELOW: **Cavalry passing the ruins of Albert Cathedral.** Albert was captured by the Allies on August 23, 1918. Atop the Cathedral stood a statue of the Virgin Mary which had become significant for the troops on both sides. Constant bombardment caused the statue to lean at a right angle. A popular myth held that when the statue finally fell, the war would end. The 'hanging Virgin' was knocked down during a British artillery bombardment in April 1918.

ABOVE: **A British soldier checks the papers of a local civilian** while searching for German deserters in June 1918. Morale among the German army was beginning to collapse as an influenza epidemic set in.

TOP RIGHT: **German dead lie abandoned in a field** as German troops withdraw from their positions on the Western Front.

MIDDLE RIGHT: **A lone Allied soldier enters Peronne Square,** shortly after the German army's withdrawal.

RIGHT: **Allied soldiers fight the Germans in Albert** in August 1918.

OPPOSITE TOP: **British soldiers in the trenches** on the outskirts of Thiepval, Sept 5, 1918.

OPPOSITE BOTTOM: **Refreshments for the wounded** after a battle during the British advance in the west.

Turkey and Bulgaria surrender

The Allies' grip on the Central Powers was tightening everywhere. Bulgaria began negotiations for peace on September 27. It was the first of Germany's allies to fall. There had been widespread resentment among the Bulgarians that they had been treated as second-class citizens by the German state, not as trusted allies. The German army had even commandeered scarce food supplies, leaving Bulgarian soldiers and civilians hungry. The Allies launched a large-scale offensive from Salonika in mid-September, and Bulgaria's desire to resist was effectively non-existent.

This was soon followed by the defeat of the once-great Ottoman Empire. General Allenby had taken Jerusalem in December 1917, but had been hampered by the redeployment of resources to the Western Front since then. He was finally ready to mount an attack once again in September 1918. Allenby tricked his opposite number, Liman von Sanders, into thinking that the point of attack would be inland – and then struck along the coast, near Megiddo. The Turkish army, which had suffered heavily from guerrilla raids organized by the Arabs assisted by T. E. Lawrence, was particularly weak there and there was a swift breakthrough. The cities of Damascus, Beirut and Aleppo fell in quick succession and, on October 30, Turkey finally surrendered.

ABOVE: **British soldiers in optimistic mood as they march to the front in Acheux, June 1918. At the beginning of the month the German army reached the Marne, as they had done in September 1914. Once again they were halted, tantalizingly short of the French capital.**

BELOW: **French towns fell to the Allies in quick succession as the Germans were beaten back or withdrew during the autumn of 1918.**

OPPOSITE LEFT: **Canadian troops in Cambrai, which fell on October 8, 1918.**

OPPOSITE RIGHT: **An Allied column marches unopposed towards the town of Cambrai in 1918. Thousands of men had lost their lives fighting for the town less than a year earlier.**

DAILY MAIL NOVEMBER 1, 1918

Turkey surrenders

Turkey has surrendered. An Allied fleet is to proceed to Constantinople and the Black Sea.

On the day that the armistice was signed, Wednesday, our Army captured the last 7,000 Turks in Mesopotamia and are marching to Mosul.

Austria has sent a white flag party to General Diaz to negotiate an armistice. The Italians, meanwhile, are advancing at a great pace, and have scooped up 50,000 prisoners

and 300 guns. The whole line is now bending. Revolutions have begun in Vienna and Budapest. The soldiers have seized control and are shouting, 'Down with the Hapsburgs.'

The Czecho-Slovaks have occupied railways on the enemy's line of retreat, and have cut the lines from Berlin to Vienna and Budapest.

British, French, and Americans attacked yesterday on the Scheldt front and gained their objectives. Our men took 1,000 prisoners.

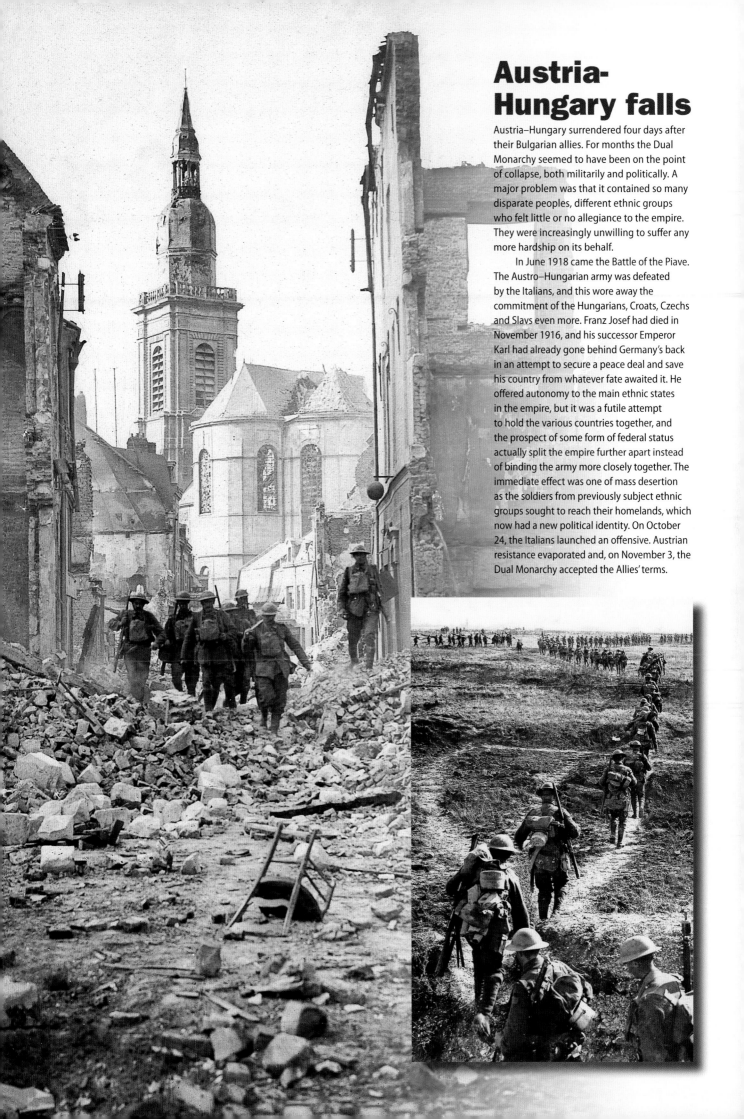

Austria-Hungary falls

Austria–Hungary surrendered four days after their Bulgarian allies. For months the Dual Monarchy seemed to have been on the point of collapse, both militarily and politically. A major problem was that it contained so many disparate peoples, different ethnic groups who felt little or no allegiance to the empire. They were increasingly unwilling to suffer any more hardship on its behalf.

In June 1918 came the Battle of the Piave. The Austro–Hungarian army was defeated by the Italians, and this wore away the commitment of the Hungarians, Croats, Czechs and Slavs even more. Franz Josef had died in November 1916, and his successor Emperor Karl had already gone behind Germany's back in an attempt to secure a peace deal and save his country from whatever fate awaited it. He offered autonomy to the main ethnic states in the empire, but it was a futile attempt to hold the various countries together, and the prospect of some form of federal status actually split the empire further apart instead of binding the army more closely together. The immediate effect was one of mass desertion as the soldiers from previously subject ethnic groups sought to reach their homelands, which now had a new political identity. On October 24, the Italians launched an offensive. Austrian resistance evaporated and, on November 3, the Dual Monarchy accepted the Allies' terms.

ENEMY IN FULL RETREAT.

Confident Predictions of French Experts.

PARIS, Tuesday.

M. Marcel Hutin writes in the *Echo de Paris*:—

The formidable battle for a decision now taking place on our front can only end in a complete victory which will make it impossible for Germany to continue the war.

Marshal Foch is not leaving it to the enemy to decide where he will fight the last battle, and this will be a Sedan on a big scale whence the enemy will retreat in haste to the other side of the Meuse.

But it is by no means certain that his withdrawal may not be turned into a disorderly retreat, or even a debacle.

Three British armies, under Generals Horne, Byng, and Rawlinson, in close liaison with our magnificent First Army,

Further progress has been made through the Forest of Mormal. Our troops took 1,000 prisoners at the capture of Le Quesnoy yesterday.

have resolutely been flung on the powerful German positions covering the roads of Avesnes, Maubeuge, and Hirson, and are following up their advance despite the desperate efforts of the Germans.

DAILY MAIL   OCTOBER 18, 1918

Capture of Ostend

Yesterday was the Allies' greatest day

The British landed at and took Ostend, captured Lille, entered Douai, and reached the outskirts of Tourcoing. The Belgians are on the edge of Bruges and the French are at Thielt, 16 miles only from Ghent.

British, Americans, and French between Le Cateau and the Oise advanced 2 miles towards the Hun line of retreat from the south and took 3,000 prisoners.

Lille's ecstasy

The Germans left Lille at 4 o'clock this morning. Our airmen saw people in the streets waving flags, and an hour after it was reported that our patrols were in the streets. The first people to enter were received with such ecstasy that it was impossible to move and escape without the help of the civic authorities. Cars were laden with flowers and gigantic bouquets; women and children crushed forward to embrace the English who entered, and cheers for England resounded down all the streets.

The German retreat is apparently general along the coast, but the enemy is holding hard for the moment in Courtrai and north of it, where our troops are fighting hard.

ABOVE: **Allied troops take control in France. Removing the German army from French soil was one of the few long-cherished objectives of the war. The collapse of the German army had come so swiftly that the Allies had given little thought to what each wanted from the peace settlement.**

LEFT: **Searching the recently bombed streets following the German withdrawal.**

Germany looks for peace

The German leadership recognized that it had now reached the end, that it was time to stop fighting a war it could no longer hope to win. It did so even before the country lost its chief ally. The new chancellor, Prince Max of Baden, sent a note to Washington on October 4 hoping to secure an armistice based on Wilson's Fourteen Points, which was considered to be the least worst option. But if Germany expected more favourable terms from America than from Britain or France, it was to be disappointed. The Germans had nothing to bargain with and had to accept whatever terms the Allies would impose, a fact not lost on President Wilson. He didn't tell the British or French of the exchanges between Washington and Berlin which the US had entered into, and Germany accepted US terms on October 27.

Marshal Foch continued to put pressure on the retreating German forces. General Pershing's American troops, supported by the French, were at the forefront of a huge offensive in the Meuse–Argonne region. This began on September 26 with the aim of capturing vital rail links, Germany's main line of communication. The American army sustained over 100,000 casualties in the next five weeks, but the final breakthrough of the First World War came on November 1.

ABOVE LEFT AND RIGHT: The war exacted a heavy toll on both sides; some 4.5 million Allies had fallen and the death toll for the Central Powers was in the region of 4 million, although the exact figure is not known.

RIGHT: Allied soldiers cheer their victory after more than four years of fighting.

OPPOSITE TOP RIGHT: The Allied delegation disembarks the train after signing the Armistice with Germany.

OPPOSITE BOTTOM RIGHT: The first military bridge is opened across the Scheldt at Tournai on November 23, 1918.

OPPOSITE LEFT: Nurses bring flowers to the grave of a fallen soldier in France.

DAILY MAIL NOVEMBER 12, 1918
Germany surrenders

The armistice was signed at 5 a.m. yesterday. The 'Cease fire' sounded at 11 a.m. The terms are such that Germany cannot fight again. She surrenders most of her arms for land, sea, and air: and she must repair and repay.

London gave itself up to joy yesterday. The scenes were beyond credence. The King toured the capital and addressed the crowds. Throughout the country and the world rejoicing is unexampled. Parliament, after acclaiming the Premier, went to St Margaret's to give thanks to God. The King attends a thanksgiving at St. Paul's to-day.

The news was announced in London at 10.20 a.m. by the Prime Minister in the following terms :-

The armistice was signed at 5 a.m. this morning, and hostilities are to cease on all fronts at 11 a.m. to-day. This was followed in half an hour by the text of Foch's 'Cease fire.'

Marshal Foch to Commander-in-Chief:

Hostilities will cease on the whole front as from November 11 at 11 o'clock (French time). The Allied troops will not, until a further order, go beyond the line reached on that date and at that hour.

GERMANY SURRENDERS.—OF

The Prime Minister made the following announcement to-day:—

The Armistice was signed at Five o'clock this morning, and hostilities are to cease on all Fronts at 11 a.m. to-day.

FOCH CALLS THE "HALT!" NO MORE SHADING OF LIGHTS.

Armistice

Ludendorff's forces had already fallen and it was only a matter of time before his entire country followed. There was revolt on the streets of Berlin and the German navy mutinied at Kiel on November 3. On November 8 Marshal Foch received an armistice delegation from Germany in a railway carriage in the forest of Compiegne. The Germans were given seventy-two hours to agree to the terms laid down, which included the introduction of democracy to the country, but the delegates didn't need that much time. The following day Kaiser Wilhelm abdicated, leaving for neutral Holland. The armistice was signed at 5.00 in the morning on November 11, and was to come into force six hours later, at 11 a.m. There was some fighting until the very last minute.

DAILY MAIL NOVEMBER 12, 1918

London's rejoicing

Utter your jubilee, steeple and spire!
Flash, ye cities in rivers of fire!
Roll and rejoice, jubilant voice!
Tennyson.

Londoners who remember 'Mafeking Night,' May 18, 1900, have always said that whatever happened in this world there could never be another Mafeking. They recanted that contention yesterday. 'Mafeking Day,' celebrated a little speck event in world history; yesterday was

world history come to its cosmic climax.

And yet, though the London scenes of yesterday in many ways recalled and surpassed those of Mafeking Day they were different. When London went delirious in the Boer War all ages took part in the carnival. On Armistice Day the middle-aged and the old walked silently, wrapped in silent joy, incommunicable reveries in a transfiguration of thankfulness and relief.

Revolution in Germany

Defeated German troops came home to a country in chaos. All the years of deprivation and hardship had failed to produce a glorious victory and mobs appeared on the streets demanding political change. The sailors' mutiny in Kiel had rapidly spread across the country and, following Kaiser Wilhelm's abdication, a new democratic government was formed – although some left-wing radicals wanted to capitalize on the public mood and engineer a Russian style revolution in Germany.

In January 1919 the communist Spartakist movement, led by Rosa Luxemburg, Leo Jogiches, Clara Zetkin, and Karl Liebknecht, staged an uprising against the new government in Berlin. Despite his left-wing leanings, the new Chancellor of Germany, Friedrich Ebert, wanted to avoid the kind of full-scale social revolution that had happened in Russia, so he called in the German army and the Freikorps (paramilitaries) to crush the rebellion. By January 13 the Spartakist leaders had been captured and executed.

Meanwhile revolution had also broken out in Bavaria, where communists had declared independence from Germany and had begun rounding-up enemy suspects and expropriating private property. Chancellor Ebert ordered the army and the Freikorps into Bavaria where they soon took control, capturing and executing an estimated 700 men and women.

TOP LEFT: **British soldiers shop at a market in Bonn during their short occupation after the war.**

TOP MIDDLE: **The Belgian Rhine Army mans a machine-gun post on the Homburg Bridge at Duisburg as a precaution against 'Red' troops invading the occupied area.**

TOP RIGHT: **A German officer, decorated with the Iron Cross, reading the proclamation of a state of siege in Danzig in April 1919. The city's predominantly German population bitterly opposed being included in a Polish state. The Treaty of Versailles made Danzig a 'Free City' under League of Nations administration.**

ABOVE: **Freikorps pose for photographers in the Wilhelmsplatz in Berlin.**

BELOW: **French troops march into Frankfurt for a brief period of occupation.**

DAILY MAIL NOVEMBER 11, 1918

Kaiser in flight

The Kaiser has abdicated and fled to Holland with the Crown Prince, and apparently also Hindenburg and the General Staff. If they went in uniform they must be interned.

He signed the abdication following a revolution in Berlin, where the Social Democrats under Ebert have hoisted the red flag on the palace and are forming a Government. Most of the army seems to have gone over to the 'Red' workers.

The courier with the armistice terms from Foch arrived at Spa, the German headquarters, only yesterday morning. Further emissaries have arrived there from Berlin and have wirelessed to the envoys at French headquarters that 'a delay of some hours' is probable. It is not clear who will sign.

Our cavalry are racing along the Brussels road. The infantry are outside Mons. Maubeuge they took on Saturday, and east of it they have captured many trains, as, farther south, have the French, who are well beyond Hirson and Mezières. France is nearly freed.

1,561st day of the war

Three weeks ago the Kaiser, aged 59 and a monarch for 30 years, called on his people to rally round him. Shortly after, he left German soil for his headquarters at Spa, in Belgium, 20 miles south of the Dutch frontier. He has not since set foot on German territory so far as is known.

Following the revolt in the Fleet and Army at home and the Republic in Bavaria, soldiers' and workmen's councils were formed in the chief cities and in many of the smaller German States.

Finally, revolution broke out in Berlin on Friday. By Saturday authority there was in the hands of the Socialists. Most of the garrison, including Guardsmen and a number of Guards and other officers, joined the revolutionaries. There was little fighting except at the cockchafers (or cadets') barracks, where some firing took place.

A large crowd proceeded to the Reichstag, where Friedrich Ebert announced that he had been charged by Prince Max of Baden to take over the Chancellorship. He is a harness maker of Heidelberg, one of the group of Socialists who supported the war so long as it was successful.

He is introducing general suffrage for men and women, who are to elect a Constituent Assembly. This will decide the form of the future Government and the position in it of the former German States. He has appealed for unity and the preservation of the food machinery. Associated with him is Scheidemann, another German Socialist leader, hitherto generally subservient to the Government. The banks have closed temporarily, to prevent a run.

It must be remembered that most of the information now available comes from the Socialists, who control the wires and the wireless.

Armistice envoys

Meantime, on Friday morning the German envoys reached Marshal Foch's headquarters and sent back a courier with the Allies' terms to German Army, which was exploding its dumps near the road he had to follow. He got to Spa only at 10.15 a.m. yesterday. More emissaries were sent thither from Berlin, and new delays seem likely.

Whose signature is valid if the armistice terms are accepted is not clear. Herr Ebert has announced that, so far as the Army is concerned, all orders must be countersigned by himself or a representative. The enemy is given till 11 this morning to say 'yes' or 'no.'

The Kaiser clung to his position almost to the last and clearly refused to abdicate till news of the revolution in Berlin arrived. Then, 'shivering and trembling,' he gave way. The Crown Prince renounced the succession, and together the two fled, accompanied, it is reported from Holland, by Hindenburg and all the staff. They did not wait to learn Foch's terms. They passed over the very ground in Belgium first violated by German troops late on August 3, 1914.

The Kaiser was in uniform and the staff was armed. Under international law they should be interned by the Dutch Government.

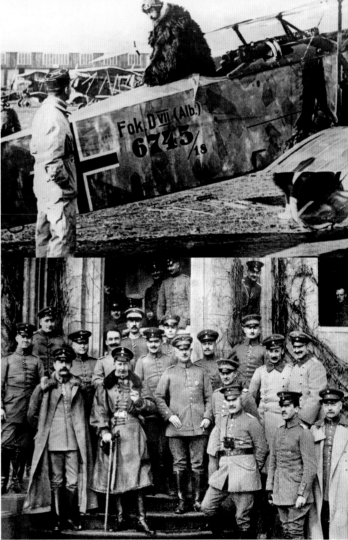

TOP: **French troops mount a machine gun on a café table in central Frankfurt as a precaution against disorder in the town.**

MIDDLE: **Germans surrender their planes to the Allies after the war.**

ABOVE: **The exiled son of Kaiser Wilhelm, ex-Crown Prince Wilhelm (holding a stick), is pictured amongst a group of supporters.**

Paris Peace Conference

It was now down to the victors to shape a workable peace, but it was to be one in which principles and ideals would inevitably clash with self-interest. The Allies had given little thought to what peace terms they would demand, largely because leading a war in which some 10 million people had lost their lives had been such an enormous task. The only coherent document that was already in existence was Woodrow Wilson's Fourteen Points.

The Paris Peace Conference opened on January 18, 1919, and President Wilson laid out his vision for a new organization to oversee conflict resolution. This League of Nations was a good idea in theory, but it was emasculated from the start when the US Senate, anxious about possible involvement in distant disputes, obstructed American membership. Nevertheless, by the end of 1919 the Covenant of the League of Nations had been incorporated into the various peace treaties and the organization set to work promoting collective security.

TOP: **Large crowds gather outside the Palace of Versailles waiting for news that the peace treaty has been signed.**

ABOVE: **Delegates gather around the conference table.**

LEFT: **The delegations from Canada and New Zealand arrive in Paris for the peace conference. Both countries sustained heavy losses in the war.**

FAR LEFT: **Australian Prime Minister Billy Hughes gives instructions to his driver in Paris. Australia sustained more than 200,000 casualties in the war.**

BELOW: **Soldiers stand guard outside the Palace of Versailles as the Treaty is signed within.**

Treaty of Versailles

There were five separate peace treaties which were signed between the Allies and each of the defeated powers. The first, and the most important, was the settlement with Germany. On June 28, 1919, the Treaty of Versailles was signed in the palace's Hall of Mirrors. The terms were severe. Alsace-Lorraine was returned to France and most of East Prussia was lost to the reunited Poland, which was also given access to the sea via the port of Danzig. Belgium and Denmark also gained territory at Germany's expense. The Saar region was to be administered by the League of Nations, and there would be a 15-year occupation of the Rhineland by the Allies. All of Germany's colonies were also forfeit. The country was not allowed to maintain a U-boat fleet nor an air force, while her army was not to exceed 100,000 men. The German High Seas Fleet was interned at Scapa Flow.

Reparations and war guilt

There were two further stipulations to the Treaty of Versailles which were even more controversial and would have severe ramifications in the future. The first was the question of reparations. France had been made to pay heavily following the Franco-Prussian War of 1870–71, and Clemenceau demanded that Germany should now be subject to similarly heavy financial penalty. France and Britain were left to settle this issue because the US did not ratify the treaty and waived all claims to reparations itself. At this point, Lloyd George and Clemenceau imposed an interim order for Germany to pay $5 billion in cash and goods, with the issue set to be reviewed at a future date. These punitive reparations, at such a high level, were impossible for the defeated country, and within four years Germany had defaulted. By the end of the 1920s it was clear that the reparations payments were completely unsustainable and they were allowed to lapse. However, the inevitable economic hardship, and the levels of resentment that this brought about, would provide an exceptionally fertile breeding ground for Adolf Hitler's National Socialist Party, established in 1921.

Secondly, the Allies insisted on adding a moral dimension to the peace settlement and a clause was included stating Germany's sole moral responsibility for the conflict. Germany could not agree with this, and the country even gathered some support among its former enemies on this point. Many high-ranking Germans, including the Kaiser, were supposed to face trial for war crimes, though in the event these never happened. Many people viewed this as overly vindictive and supported the appeasement of Nazi Germany when it went about reversing the treaty in the period before the Second World War.

TOP RIGHT: **The Big Four at Versailles. From left to right: Prime Minister Vittorio Orlando of Italy, Prime Minister David Lloyd George of Great Britain, Prime Minister Georges Clemenceau of France and President Woodrow Wilson of the United States.**

MIDDLE RIGHT: **German representatives listen to Clemenceau's speech during a meeting at the Trianon Palace Hotel in Versailles where the Peace Treaty was officially handed over to them.**

ABOVE RIGHT: **President Wilson doffs his cap in greeting outside the Trianon Palace Hotel in Versailles.**

ABOVE LEFT: **The Peace Treaty is signed in the Hall of Mirrors in Louis XIV's monumental Palace of Versailles.**

Treaty of Saint Germain

A new Republic of Austria was created in the Treaty of Saint-Germain, signed on September 10, 1919, and Italy regained some of her former territory. The disparate Austro–Hungarian empire was broken up, and the independence of Czechoslovakia, Poland and Hungary was also recognized. Serbia's pre-war wish for a Slav state could also be granted. The Kingdom of Serbs, Croats and Slovenes – later renamed Yugoslavia – was created, with Alexander I as its first head of state. However, this new country also included Macedonians, Bosnians and Albanians, a volatile ethnic mix that would create tensions and, 70 years later, lead to war and the break up of the country.

The settlement with Bulgaria came with the Treaty of Neuilly which was signed on November 27, 1919; Bulgaria ceded land to Greece, Romania and Yugoslavia, including its outlet to the Aegean Sea. The Treaty of Trianon, signed on June 4, 1920, reduced Hungary to a fraction of its former size. Romania got Transylvania, for which it had gone to war, while Czechoslovakia and Yugoslavia also benefited.

Treaty of Sèvres

The final document in all these peace agreements, the Treaty of Sèvres, was signed with Turkey on August 10, 1920. Mesopotamia and Palestine both became British mandates while Syria became a French mandate, and Turkey also lost territory to Greece and Italy. This particular treaty fell apart very soon. A nationalist movement led by Mustafa Kemal (Ataturk) resented the conciliatory approach adopted by the Ottoman Sultan Mehmed VI, and Kemal swept to power on a promise of recovering some of the country's lost territory. On July 24, 1923, following a bitter struggle against Greece, the Treaty of Lausanne was signed. Turkey regained Thrace and Smyrna, which had been allocated to Greece under the Treaty of Sèvres three years earlier.

TOP RIGHT: A spoil of war; a German U-Boat lies in the River Thames close to the Houses of Parliament in December 1918.

the peace treaty was signed. They will take the places of men awaiting demobilization.

BELOW: The 21st Canadian Infantry Battalion crosses a bridge over the River Rhine at Bonn.

TOP LEFT: Members of the Women's Legion Army Service Corps leave London bound for France on the same day

LEFT: General Pershing, commander of American forces in Europe, gets a hero's welcome when he visits London after the war.

Resentments grow

The peace treaties caused much ill feeling, and not just in those countries which had experienced financial and territorial losses. Italy thought it should have been given a greater share of the spoils and Benito Mussolini formed a new political party, Fasci di Combattimento, in 1919, with the chief aim of restoring the country's national pride. One method of achieving this was by the acquisition of new territory, and Italy looked to Africa to provide this.

Internally, post-conflict Europe was far from being settled and peaceful; it was bedevilled by border disputes and economic hardship. The redrawn map of the continent left all of the newly formed states with disaffected minorities, though Germany remained the greatest problem. The country had not been dismembered in the way the Austro–Hungarian and Ottoman empires had, though it had been badly injured. The terms of the peace agreements were harsh enough to provoke an acrimonious response but Germany was not permanently shackled in the way that France had wanted – as, indeed, future events would show. Germany was admitted to the League of Nations in 1926. Adolf Hitler assumed power seven years later and one of his earliest acts was to withdraw from it; he then repudiated the military constraints of the Treaty of Versailles and the country embarked on a massive rearmament programme. The apparent vindictiveness of the 1919 Versailles treaty was instrumental in Hitler's rise to power, and in the events which followed. Some prescient individuals were already warning – as early as 1919 – that war had not been concluded, only suspended for the moment. The so-called 'war to end all wars' would eventually be widely regarded as being a prelude to the Second World War.

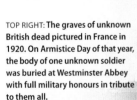

TOP RIGHT: **The graves of unknown British dead pictured in France in 1920. On Armistice Day of that year, the body of one unknown soldier was buried at Westminster Abbey with full military honours in tribute to them all.**

MIDDLE RIGHT: **Repatriated British prisoners of war arrive home to tea and biscuits in London.**

ABOVE LEFT: **General Pershing pictured visiting the men busy building 'Pershing Stadium' at Joinville, France, in June 1919 and (above centre) arriving in Paris.**

ABOVE RIGHT: **The emergence of the 'special relationship': President Wilson with King George V after the war.**

RIGHT: **Veterans of the Ypres campaigns march past the town's famous Cloth Hall, May 21, 1920.**

Acknowledgements

The photographs in this book are from the archives of the *Daily Mail*.
Particular thanks to Steve Torrington, Alan Pinnock and all the staff.

Thanks also to Alison Gauntlett, Lauren Oing, Michael Quiello, Bradford Swann,
Laurence Socha, Christopher Sullivan, Patricia Annunziata,
Caitlin Gildea, Cliff Salter and Richard Betts